APPRECIATIVE INQUIRY
in the
Catholic Church

BY SUSAN STAR PADDOCK

Dedication: to the Sacred Heart of Jesus
This book was completed 5/31/2003, the Feast Day of
The Visitation of the Virgin Mary to St. Elizabeth.

Appreciative Inquiry in the Catholic Church
ISBN 0966537343
Copyright 2003 Susan Star Paddock
All rights reserved
Editor: Sue Annis Hammond
Designer: Alisann Marshall
Design Assistant: Krystal Neufeld
Copy Editors: Dana Joseph, Susan Armstrong
Editorial Assistant: Sarah Shields

Note: The Scripture quotations contained herein are from the *New Revised Standard Version Bible*, copyright 1989 by the Division of Christian Education of the National Council of Churches of Christ in the U.S.A., and are used with permission. All rights reserved. Oxford University Press.

Photographs were shot on location in Northern Italy by Alisann Marshall ©2003.

Thin Book Publishing Co
PO Box 260608
Plano TX 75026-0608
www.thinbook.com
888.316.9544 (phone)
888.331.8966 (fax)

C O N T E N T S

CHAPTER 1

APPRECIATIVE INQUIRY

a Path to

Positive Change

APPRECIATIVE INQUIRY
A Path to Positive Change

In October 2001 managers from Catholic Relief Services joined in an important dialogue with 600 leaders from many other non-profit, government, and business organizations. They had gathered in Baltimore for the First International Conference on Appreciative Inquiry. From American Baptist Ministries to British Airways, from the Red Cross to Roadway Express, the diverse presenters and attendees represented at least 20 countries. Although the meeting occurred just three weeks after the 9/11 terrorist attacks, registration did not drop, but actually rose in the days leading up to the conference. At a time when the need for hope and healing was greatest, people were choosing to learn more about a highly effective strategy for intentional change.

In troubled times it's easy to focus on what's wrong, but the usual problem-solving approach to life often provides more discouragement than effectiveness. Our brows knit in concentration on the negative, while the answers to our problems elude us. Appreciative Inquiry (AI) reveals that those answers are often already present in our experiences. AI helps us explore when things have worked well, when things were at their best, and identify the causes of success.

Great teachers know that maximum learning comes from catching children doing something right and building on the skills that are already present. Appreciative Inquiry asks participants to do just that, to notice what's going right, to make it visible, and to build on that wisdom. The most important underlying assumption of Appreciative Inquiry is the belief that there is already excellence in all communities and systems. By looking for, displaying, discussing, and analyzing what already works, we can help an organization rise to greater heights. The power of the process lies in building on strengths instead of attempting to combat weaknesses. AI theorists believe that people and organizations, like plants that move toward the light, grow in a positive direction when light becomes evident. When Jesus said, *"You are the light of the world"* (Matthew 5:14)[1] he asked us to lift up that light and not hide it *"under a bushel"* of negativity. St. Paul advised just that for the Philippians. *"Finally beloved, whatever is true, whatever is honorable, whatever is just, whatever is pure, whatever is pleasing, whatever is commendable, if there is any excellence and if there is anything worthy of praise, think about these things"* (Philippians 4:8).

WHAT IS APPRECIATIVE INQUIRY?

Appreciative Inquiry is a philosophy and toolset created in the context of a discipline called Organizational Behavior or Organization Development (OD). Organization Development departments in the business, psychology, or education schools of many universities study how people behave in organizations. Two such schools co-sponsored the Baltimore Conference and are key incubators of the AI philosophy. They are: The Weatherhead School of Management at Case Western Reserve University[2], where AI was conceived by David Cooperrider and others in the early eighties, and Benedictine University in Illinois. Professors in these two schools have inspired and coached many of the people mentioned in this book.

Appreciative Inquiry is a departure from the way OD consultants have historically studied organizations. Typically, they have employed a medical diagnostic model: define the presenting problem, analyze the causes, and fix the problem. In such traditional problem-solving the best outcome is an elimination of the problem.

TRADITIONAL OD PROCESS	APPRECIATIVE INQUIRY
Define the problem	Search for best practices that already exist
Fix what's broken	Amplify what is working
Work incrementally	Full system, fast cycle change
Focus on decay	Focus on life-giving forces
What problems are you having?	*What is working well around here?* [3]

For example, in a medical setting, a patient treated by diagnosis and prescription may become symptom-free, but still have serious health risks from lifestyle choices. In a holistic wellness approach, the medical professional looks at the whole person, just as the Appreciative Inquiry approach looks at the whole system. To achieve wellness, a person or system must look within to deeply examine core values and priorities, and make choices to proceed based on the healthiest or highest values. At the end of an AI, not only does the system know what it does well, it also has created goals and plans for how to be "more" than it was before. By shifting a worldview from deficit-based analysis and planning — "what's wrong; who is to blame; why have we failed; how can we treat the illness?" — to a strength-based model of action research — "what works around here; what might be; what should be; let's innovate what will be," AI infuses organizations with new vision and life.

That sense of rejuvenation is fundamental to the process. Appreciative Inquiry focuses on discovering what David Cooperrider calls the life-giving forces of an organization. As a practicing psychotherapist and organization consultant, I was attracted to AI's power to effect positive change and rejuvenate organizations. I've successfully used AI with individuals, families, colleges, businesses, nonprofits, and faith communities.

In 2002, I saw an opportunity for AI to play a healing role in my adopted spiritual home, the Catholic Church. With the widespread media coverage of the sex-abuse cases, I realized the Church was at a crossroads. Catholics could pursue the usual diagnostic course of analyzing what went wrong, or we could use the energy created by crisis for an inquiry into what is right with our church. We would not ignore the ramifications of the crisis, or excuse anyone's behavior. We would simply choose, during this time of trial to rediscover the good that continues to be generated every day within the Church. We can amplify the best of who we are, envision together the Church we need to be and build for the future. We could move beyond a focus on symptoms to a deeper dialogue about the life-giving forces of the church.

Such dialogue would mirror the earliest beginnings of the Christian Church, when disheartened disciples, hiding out in fear and grief, told transformative stories to one another. As Jesus' friends shared the news of the Resurrection and spoke about high points of their life with the Lord, they grew in courage and confidence. They became more deeply aligned with their highest vision. Their being together in prayer and fellowship, reflecting on the peak experiences of their conversions, surely helped them to be open to the presence of the Holy Spirit in their midst. Deep sharing transformed pain into peace and the power to follow where the Spirit led.

I wondered if Appreciative Inquiry was already being used in the Catholic Church and if so, where? I'm happy to report that there are some wonderful examples to share from Catholic organizations as well as other faith communities. The more I spoke with people, the more I realized that AI is philosophically aligned with the messages and mission of Christ. With AI, the means by which results are achieved match the emphasis of Christian social teachings on the profound worth and dignity of every human being. AI produces practical results, and most important, its essentially loving means are as important as the ends.

I hope you will be inspired to use some of the ideas so generously shared by the people in the book. I've listed names and resources for further information. It is my goal that this book will give you an idea of things you could do tomorrow that might shine the light on what gives life to our church.

HOW TO DO AN APPRECIATIVE INQUIRY

Several good books explain Appreciative Inquiry in depth (see Resources). This chapter provides an overview of the process so you can understand the various examples in the rest of the book. AI is a generative theory, which means it is developing as people use it. Various people have created models of the process in order to teach it to others. David Cooperrider proposes a: "Four D" process:

Discover: "Appreciate what is."
Dream: "Imagine what might be."
Design: "Determine what should be."
Deliver: "Create what will be."

Authors Jane Watkins and Bernard J. Mohr insert one more "D" — for Definition — at the beginning of the process in their book *Appreciative Inquiry: Change at the Speed of Imagination*[4]. Here is a summary of the five steps from their book:

1. DEFINE: *Choose the focus of the inquiry*

Someone will introduce key leaders to Appreciative Inquiry. Often the leadership creates a representative small team to learn about Appreciative Inquiry, to start conversations to identify the topics of the inquiry and to manage the project as a whole. Dr. Cathy Royal, co-editor of *Lessons from the Field: Applying Appreciative Inquiry*[5] says "AI begins with choosing a topic by asking 'What do we want to see more of?' and 'What do we want to have happen here?' This is a critical first step because what you focus on will guide the dialogue for the entire organization." Royal also says categorically, "The energy follows the inquiry, so it is important to choose well."

2. DISCOVER: *Inquire into stories of life-giving forces*

Discover has two sub-steps. First the team develops affirmative questions to use in interviews with as many stakeholders as possible, at all levels of the organization. The interviews are usually one-on-one, and can last from 20 minutes to an hour or more. The answers, often in the form of stories, are the raw data on which the rest of the work is based. Because topics of inquiry differ, there aren't "standard" questions[6]. Some basic questions have, however, been used or adapted by many practitioners. Here are a few sample questions:

Historical: Inquire about times when things were at their best, or when an individual had a peak experience. For example: Tell me a story about a time when you felt most alive and proud of being a Catholic?

Inner-directed: Inquire about the strengths an individual brings to the situation or about core factors or values that determine the essence of who we are. For example: God gifts each of us with certain abilities. Without being humble, what strengths have you been given that enable you to contribute positively to our parish? What is the single most important thing our parish has contributed to your life? What do you value most about yourself as a Catholic?

Future-oriented: Inquire about wishes for what you'd like to see more of in the future. For example: If you could imagine or transform our parish in any way you wished, what one to three things would you like to see happen to enhance its life and vitality?

Such heartfelt questions quickly establish a sense of intimacy and lead people to consider core values. More significantly, they reflect a desire to see and appreciate more deeply the goodness of God's creation.

The stories from the interviews are then used in the second sub-step of Discovery: data analysis. With as many of the people who were interviewed as possible, the stories from the interviews are shared so that the core themes among the stories surface. In large group settings or small teams, people talk about what those themes mean to them as individuals and as a parish. The group selects the themes that, if amplified, would enhance the church's future vitality.

3. DREAM: *Create shared images for a preferred future*

At this step the group begins to ask itself what the future would look like based on the core themes and the representative stories revealed in the second step. They ask themselves "If all these themes were fully realized every day, what would our parish look like? Based on these reflections, what is God calling us to be?" Typically there are two stages in the dreaming phase. The first stage recognizes the value of play and image in the creative process. Participants are urged to begin metaphorically, expressing a desirable future through visual images, skits, poems, and songs.

In the second stage, these vibrant images are translated into words. Participants write statements called "provocative propositions" in affirmative and present-tense language, as in *"You are the salt of the earth"* (Matthew 5:13). These statements are based on historical reality, the best practices previously discovered. They describe the agreed-upon preferred image of the future and stretch our ideas of what is possible. They are like vision statements that people grow into, or value statements that guide the rest of the planning because they state what the preferred future looks like.

4. DESIGN: *Find innovative ways to create that future*

The dreams of Step 3 are designed into practicality by examining all the people and processes that make up the system as a whole. These exploratory conversations consider how living the shared vision would impact members, partners, councils, boards, hierarchy, volunteers, ministries, organizational structure, governance, the environment, and the sustainability of the organization. The desired future often requires new actions, relationships, and roles.

5. DELIVER: *Implement the changes*

In Step 5 the design is translated into action. Each person looks within and commits to deliver the part of the future they are most concerned with. As the actions are carried out, people continue the conversation about what is going right and the wishes for the preferred future. AI is often an iterative process; one inquiry leads to another as people re-define their preferred future.

Through these five steps, Appreciative Inquiry creates effective large-scale change as shown in chapter 3, the case study on Catholic Relief Services. When there isn't time or a commitment to large-scale change, an "appreciative approach" is often used as we will see in many of this book's examples. The key is to keep close to the philosophy of affirmation underlying the process. As Brother Larry Fidelus of the Carmelite Brothers says, the Appreciative Inquiry philosophy is a quest to see that "the glass is half-full and how do we make it more full?"

CHAPTER 2

COMPATIBILITY

The Link Between

Appreciative Inquiry

and the Catholic Church

COMPATIBILITY
The Link Between Appreciative Inquiry and the Catholic Church

CATHOLIC SOCIAL TEACHING

Catholic Social Teaching, sometimes called Catholicism's "best kept secret,"[1] is a collection of writings on contemporary issues found in papal statements, conferences of Bishops, and Vatican II documents from the last 100 years. It emphasizes building what it terms "right" relationships with all people — inclusive, just, loving, and respectful — through the pursuit of peace, justice, and the elimination of poverty and inequality.

Catholic Social Teaching and Appreciative Inquiry share many values. While Catholic Social Teaching is derived from Scripture and religious tradition, and AI is derived from the scientific and experiential analysis of social and biological systems, both arrive at similar conclusions about the dignity of persons, our interdependence, and the necessity for full participation and inclusion in society's processes.

For example, themes of Catholic Social Teaching as articulated by the US Conference of Catholic Bishops include the following statements:[2] "We believe that every person is precious, that people are more important than things, and that the measure of every institution is whether it threatens or enhances the life and dignity of the human person. We believe people have a right and duty to participate in society, seeking together the common good and well-being of all, especially the poor and vulnerable."

The Bishops also emphasized the importance of solidarity: "We are our brothers' and sisters' keepers, wherever they live ... one human family ... Learning to practice the virtue of solidarity means that 'loving our neighbor' has global dimensions in an interdependent world."

David Cooperrider, a key Appreciative Inquiry theorist, delineates similar values when he states, "Appreciative Inquiry is based on a reverence for life." He believes AI incorporates three universal needs of all humans: the need for Exceptionality, Essentiality, and Equality of voice. He explains the three Es as follows:[3]

"By exceptionality I mean that every human being is an exception to the rule — no one has ever been born quite like you and no one in the future will ever again be quite like you ... We all have a basic human want to be recognized as "essential" to any human group we belong to ... Finally I think all human beings in every group they are a part of feel some sense of equality, especially equality of voice. We all have a desire to be able to share, without censorship, our hopes and visions of the true, the good and the possible."

This recognition of the essential value and equality of every human being is one meaning of Jesus' words, in Matthew (25:40) *"Truly I tell you, just as you did it to one of the least of these who are members of my family, you did it to me."* St. Paul's discourse on the Body of Christ also emphasizes the importance of every individual within the group. *"As it is there are many members yet one body. The eye cannot say to the hand, 'I have no need of you,' nor again the head to the feet, 'I have no need of you.' On the contrary, the members of the body that seem to be weaker are indispensable. If one member suffers, all suffer together with it; if one member is honored, all rejoice together with it."* (I Corinthians 12:20-26)

Catholic Social Teaching and Appreciative Inquiry advocates see that images and attitudes can be changed through dialogue, with the hoped-for result of just relationships across cultures. After taking office during Vatican II, Pope Paul VI emphasized the importance of dialogue within the church and with all of humanity.

POPE PAUL VI ON DIALOGUE

In his first Encylical, *Ecclesium Suam*[4] ("Our Church"), 1964, Pope Paul VI wrote: *"The Church needs to reflect upon itself and to become aware of its own extraordinary vitality. It must strive to gain a fuller understanding of itself if it is to do what it has to do and bring to the world the message of salvation and brotherly love. To this internal drive of charity which seeks expression in the external gift of charity, We will apply the word dialogue. Here, then... is the noble origin of this dialogue: in the mind of God Himself... Indeed, the whole history of man's salvation is one long, varied dialogue, which marvelously begins with God and which He prolongs with men in so many different ways... But it seems to Us that the sort of relationship for the Church to establish with the world should be dialogue...demanded nowadays...by the maturity man has reached in this day and age. Be he religious or not, his secular education has enabled him to think and speak, and conduct a dialogue with dignity. Dialogue, therefore, is a recognized method of the apostolate. It is a way of making spiritual contact."*

Descriptions of the positive affect of Appreciative Inquiry parallel Pope Paul VI's description of an ideal dialogue, when he wrote,

"It would indeed be a disgrace if our dialogue were marked by arrogance, the use of bared words or offensive bitterness. What gives it its authority is the

fact that it affirms the truth, shares with others the gifts of charity, is itself an example of virtue, avoids peremptory language, makes no demands. It is peaceful, has no use for extreme methods, is patient under contradiction and inclines towards generosity."

Many people describe Appreciative Inquiry as a "privilege of listening and being listened to" which parallels Pope Paul VI's description of listening:

"Then, before speaking, we must take great care to listen not only to what men say, but more especially to what they have it in their hearts to say. Only then will we understand them and respect them, and even, as far as possible, agree with them...How greatly we desire that this dialogue with Our own children may be conducted with the fullness of faith, with charity, and with dynamic holiness. May it be of frequent occurrence and on an intimate level. May it be open and responsive to all truth, every virtue, every spiritual value that goes to make us the heritage of Christian teaching. We want it to be sincere. We want it to be an inspiration to genuine holiness. We want it to show itself ready to listen to the variety of views which are expressed in the world today. We want it to be the sort of dialogue that will make Catholics virtuous, wise, unfettered, fair-minded and strong."

AN EARLY ADAPTER

Father Gregorio Banaga Jr., C.M.[5] was influenced by Pope Paul VI and his emphasis on dialogue as a spiritual discipline. Yet when he first attended a workshop on Appreciative Inquiry at Loyola University, he was skeptical of the "touchy-feely" methodology and feared it would sugarcoat real issues instead of confronting them head-on. Fr. Banaga describes himself as naturally "logical, critical, and analytical," with a mind that automatically gravitates to the "default mode" of looking for problems and solutions. It was during Ph.D. coursework in organizational behavior at Case Western Reserve University, with David Cooperrider as an advisor, that Banaga began to look at the world through a different lens.

Banaga was serving as spiritual director of the Philippine American Ministry in the Diocese of Cleveland in 1996 when he decided to experiment with Appreciative Inquiry. He used it for strategic planning on the occasion of the 20-year celebration of that ministry. His small team of six people interviewed members of the 700-family organization. He was interested in knowing whether people who used the methodology would be changed by it. He concluded that the tools we use do change us. "Methodology affects worldview," he says. His planning team members "were changed by the method. Their perspective of life became more positive."

Banaga realized that focusing on the negative in analysis is no more logical than focusing on the positive, and that we shape our view of reality by what we focus on. "Life is different when you focus on the positive," he says. "There is more affirmation, more possibilities, and more hope. Isn't that what the Church is all about? The role of the Church is to give hope."

Reflecting on that first project led Banaga to contribute the chapter *A Spiritual Path to Organizational Renewal* to the book *Lessons from the Field*.[6] He wrote, "Appreciative Inquiry does not turn a blind eye on 'negative' situations or 'deficit-oriented' realities in organizations; it does not substitute a 'rosy' and 'romantic' picture for an 'objective' and 'realistic' one. It accepts these realities for what they are — areas in need of conversion and transformation. All intentionality shifts the focus of the inquiry and intervention to those realities that are sources of vitality and that manifest the marvels of God within an organization." He concluded, "AI is much more than a technical and methodological tool for organizational analysis and effectiveness. Undertaken in a spirit of faith and informed by Christian Scriptures, it can become a powerful means for corporate spiritual renewal."

THE POWER OF AI FOR SPIRITUAL RENEWAL

DEEPENING DISCIPLINE

Fr. Banaga, who is also the coordinator of continuing formation for his religious community, believes that Appreciative Inquiry is a philosophy with deep roots in Scripture and Catholic theology. In a spiritual retreat he conducted for diocesan priests, he explained how AI embodies the disciplines of appreciation, dialogue, and planning, all of which enhance the Christian path. In Fr. Banaga's experience, Appreciative Inquiry deepens and enriches the practice of these spiritual disciplines.

SHARING PROFOUNDLY

Appreciative Inquiry provides an opportunity for the profound sharing of positive life stories among believers. Rick Krivanka,[7] Gail Roussey, and David DeLambo, staff members of the Pastoral Planning Office at the Diocese of Cleveland have worked with AI for the past several years. For Krivanka, AI's compatibility with the Gospel comes from the intimate sharing that is implicit in the process. "The heart of the church is the Good News," Krivanka says. "Well what is the Good News? The Good News is in the stories of God's presence and grace at work in the lives of people. The wonderful connection with AI is that it provides a way to focus on what the Good News is today in the life of our different communities, and it encourages people to really hold this up and talk about it in a way that brings out the joy and meaning of their stories. There is no other methodology I know of that goes so directly parallel to the life and movement of the Church, namely the focus on 'Tell the Good News.' The very imagery of AI affirms that no matter what else is happening, we have the Good News of God-with-us."

Gail Roussey agrees. She believes that the one-on-one interview process in Appreciative Inquiry uniquely complements the Gospel and the work of the Catholic Church. "As an individual experience it's unlike anything else that people are likely to go through," she says. "People don't tend to sit down and talk intimately about matters of faith unless they participate in a small faith-sharing community. And even there the format is likely to provide more give and take, while the AI format is structured so that one person is speaking and one person listens for 45 minutes about matters that are deeply personal concerning the individual's faith journey. This type of listening doesn't happen that often unless a person has a spiritual director. So it's very powerful for the individuals involved."

BUILDING FAITH

David DeLambo feels that the Appreciative Inquiry interview is an important tool for building faith. "The dynamic between the interviewer and the interviewee is a key experience," DeLambo says. "The person being interviewed is undergoing a moment of faith formation where they are trying to connect the Gospel with their lives. The interviewer is being evangelized by God in the presence of this person's life. The same thing happens in a small faith community. The individual is moved by the power of hearing how God works in others' lives. The interviews alone have great merit even if there were no further organizational development."

Krivanka concurs, "Some people being interviewed will say, 'I've just not thought about these things and it's so important to talk about them.' One elderly couple that interviewed as a team at St. Bernard Parish in Akron, Ohio, told me, 'I just want to tell you that doing these interviews is one of the most wonderful things we've ever done in our lives.' Another, from St. Mary Parish in Hudson, Ohio, told me, 'Rick, we had no clue what an incredible parish this is. We had no clue how things were really going in the faith lives of the people and how much this parish really means to people. If we did nothing else but the interviews it would have been enough because of the impact it has had on our parish and our people.' If you asked people what they thought about St. Mary's, most would say that St. Mary's is a dynamic parish, but we made a deeper discovery that there is so much more life and faith than we see on the surface."

CHANGING CULTURE

Rick Krivanka believes that when you begin the Appreciative Inquiry process, you create a change in the culture within the organization to become more life centered. "Ideally it changes the discourse — what people talk about and the images that shape their lives," he says. "The plan is not as important as whether we change the culture and the discourse, capturing the deeper spirituality."

For example, Krivanka notes that some of the most eloquent statements of what it means to be Church and what Eucharist means to people surfaced at meetings when people reflected on their interviews. "One man said, 'The Eucharist is the source and summit of my life. It is the foundation of everything.' He was quoting a Vatican II document on Eucharist, not as a document of what we're supposed to aspire to, but as a testament to what truly happens in his life. And he said it with such earnestness that there was no question about it. This was a moment of proclaiming the Good News."

FULFILLING HOPES OF VATICAN II

Krivanka emphasized that "AI is meant to focus on what most inspires you and gives you hope, and what greater dreams can come forth out of this." As noted in the discussion on Catholic Social Teaching, AI promotes inclusiveness and trust with the belief that each one of us is of immense value and can contribute ideas, dreams, and strategies. This appreciative emphasis on just relationships also mirrors the best hopes of Vatican II. The Dogmatic Constitution of the Catholic Church speaks about just relationships by articulating the equality of laity (defined as "all the faithful") and clergy in Lumen Gentium[8]:

"As the laity through the divine choice have Christ as their brother, who, though Lord of all, came not to be served but to serve (cf. Mt. 20:28) they also have as brothers those in the sacred ministry who by teaching, by sanctifying and by ruling with the authority of Christ so nourish the family of God that the new commandment of love may be fulfilled by all. As St. Augustine very beautifully puts it: 'When I am frightened by what I am to you, then I am consoled by what I am with you. To you I am the bishop, with you I am a Christian. The first is an office, the second a grace; the first a danger, the second salvation.' Gathered together in the People of God and established in the one Body of Christ under one head, the laity — no matter who they are — have, as living members, the vocation of applying to the building up of the Church and to its continual sanctification all the powers which they have received from the goodness of the Creator and from the grace of the Redeemer..."

Appreciative Inquiry can help realize the dream of Vatican II. Because it is philosophically aligned with the intentions of the Church, AI can help release the gifts and power of the Body of Christ.

CHAPTER 3

REACHING OUT

Using Appreciative Inquiry

to Build Relationships

and Community

REACHING OUT

Using Appreciative Inquiry to Build Relationships and Community

CATHOLIC RELIEF SERVICES

Catholic Relief Services (CRS) organizational improvement efforts provide a good example of how Appreciative Inquiry works when embraced as a large-scale change process. In a two-year process detailed in their excellent guide to relationship building called *The Partnership Toolbox: A Facilitator's Guide to Partnership Dialogue*,[1] CRS examined itself through an appreciative lens.

Since 1943 CRS has focused on international development and relief activities, working entirely through partners such as local Catholic dioceses and compatible non-governmental organizations. Many of the relationships between CRS and local partners have spanned 30 years or more and have changed significantly during that time. In 1996 CRS began to revitalize itself. The agency wanted to view all of its programs through the "justice lens" of Catholic Social Teaching while looking at ways to (1) improve the quality of partnership relationships and (2) synchronize those partnerships with Catholic Social Teaching. Additionally, CRS wanted to use a methodology that itself reflected the type of life-enhancing relationship embodied in the justice lens.

CRS learned about Appreciative Inquiry from a CRS partner organization that had used it successfully in Bangladesh. Seeing that Appreciative Inquiry worked with the people it served encouraged CRS to use it as the method by which all levels of the organization and its partners could reflect together on just and quality partnerships. With the help of Claudia Liebler of The GEM Initiative[2] CRS used the classic Cooperrider "4-D" Model of a complete AI process.

DISCOVER

The Discover step began with a two-day training session with CRS staff and representatives from partner organizations at CRS' Baltimore headquarters. In response to this training, CRS decided on a worldwide inquiry to explore three challenges: improving the quality of partnerships between CRS and its local partners; generating agency-wide learning; and encouraging a joint learning process to design, document, and disseminate innovative models of capacity building and partnership development. The Discovery phase allowed both groups to think about the life-giving forces in their partnership — what made it last and where it could be improved. It was also a time to resolve any outstanding hurt and misunderstandings in a spirit of reconciliation. The following questions used in this phase included:

BEST EXPERIENCE OF A PARTNERSHIP[3]

Tell me about a high point — a time when you felt you were involved in a really good partnership, a time that stands out as significant, meaningful, mutually empowering, or particularly effective in terms of results achieved. Share the story. What made it a good partnership? How were you involved? What were the key learnings?

VALUES OF HIGH-QUALITY PARTNERSHIPS

1. Yourself: Without being humble, what do you value the most about yourself [in terms of what] things you bring to building high-quality partnerships?

2. Your Society and Culture: Every society or culture has its own unique qualities, beliefs, traditions, or capabilities that prepare us for building good partnership relations. What two to three things about your culture or society are you most proud about in relation to qualities that might enhance or help build good partnerships? Can you share a story about your culture that illustrates its best partnership qualities?

3. Your Organization: What currently are your organization's best practices, skills, values, methods, or traditions that make it ready to be a good partner organization?

4. Core Value: As you think about what it takes to build high-quality partnerships, especially across organizations from different cultures, what is the core life-giving factor in such partnerships, without which good partnerships would not be possible?

THREE WISHES

If you had three wishes for this partnership, what would they be?

Meg Kinghorn, a former CRS staff member who was involved in the process, says the questions were well-received. "It has made a big difference in our partnerships to actually focus on 'What are the life-giving qualities? What is the goodness of the history of our working together?' rather than the traditional question, 'What are your complaints about us?' Our partners say, 'Finally, you're talking about what's good in our lives, instead of what's wrong with us!'"

DREAM AND DESIGN

Dream and Design began when CRS asked people to imagine their partnership five years in the future, when it had reached a point that was exciting, effective, and excellent in every respect. They made the visualization practical by asking everyone to imagine the details of what would be going on and to discover what people would be doing differently?[4] After the imaginative dreaming, partners worked together on plans to put into operation a set of provocative propositions, which they refined and called "CRS Partnership Principles." The eleven principles included the following:

• "CRS and its partners maximize community participation in all aspects of programming to ensure community ownership of, and decision-making within, the development process."

• "CRS promotes mutual transparency regarding capacities, constraints, and resources."

• "All of CRS' partnerships assign responsibility for decision-making and implementation to a level as close as possible to the people whom decisions will affect."

RESULTS

Catholic Relief Services experienced the spiraling effect of AI, with one inquiry leading to another on a related subject. CRS realized that the information it received from its external partners was a call to look inwardly at its systems, policies, and procedures and to explore how to make them congruent with the emerging partnership principles. As a result, CRS and GEM organized a new AI, beginning with a three-day workshop focused on inquiry questions such as "How do the Partnership Principles impact the way CRS conducts its business?"

The data from the partnership meetings and the second inquiry fed into two international summits held in Baltimore in 1998 and 2000. From 1998 to 2001 similar local, then regional, meetings led to major strategy summits looking at program quality, management quality, emergency services, education, and micro-finance. These meetings in turn contributed to the 2001 World Summit. The strategic process that began with a decision to look through the justice lens eventually involved 4,000 staff in more than 80 countries, all addressing the same question: "What should CRS be doing in the New World?"

The Partnership Toolbox was only one of the outcomes of the Deliver phase. The real prize was greatly improved relationships with partners. CRS learned that when people begin the process of talking to each other in new and constructive ways, they are able to build improved relationships. GEM's Claudia Liebler felt the program was successful in many ways and says: "We created an agency-wide dialogue. Positive changes were made in relationships and discussions were held with staff from all parts of the agency on how to make the social architecture of CRS more congruent with the principles of partnership. There was a great deal of interest in adapting systems and processes to be more partner friendly."

Although CRS has not "officially" adopted Appreciative Inquiry, Kinghorn feels that "AI permeates the CRS approach to planning. Where once the criteria for success were more technical, now our vision of program quality is not strictly technical quality, but involves relationships. CRS says our mission is to 'build a just world.' Justice is right relationships as defined by Catholic Social Teaching. Our mission is not to eliminate poverty or to increase crop yields but to build right relationships. It's a positive model. Our new definition of program quality is that quality programs transform lives, structures, and relationships." Kinghorn says that instead of asking, "is this child's food secure, they now ask questions like: Is that child's relationship to her parents secure? Is her teacher's relationship to the mayor secure? How is the mayor's relationship to the father, to the governor? Are relationships right in that context, in an ever-widening circle of relationships? When there is poverty or an emergency in a world with justice, people work together," Kinghorn says.

Another CRS employee, Jennifer Nazaire, goes on to say that, "Appreciative Inquiry will continue to be a part of how the agency does things— in whole, or in part — and as an underlying ethos." Since staffers have seen its value over so many years, they use certain aspects of the formal process a great deal. "There's always a tendency to think about Appreciative Inquiry as a way to do visioning and planning, but rarer for us to go through the whole AI cycle," Nazaire says. "It's more a part of our consciousness to look for the positive and build on that. That's what most people have taken away — the philosophy. That will continue to be a part of the way we see, do, and feel things." Appreciative Inquiry has been effective for CRS because it works quickly in all cultures, reduces resistance, and increases motivation. At CRS, the newly examined relationship possibilities bring Catholic Social Teaching to life. As Kinghorn puts it, "Appreciative Inquiry mirrors the old, old teachings of the church. It's not new. It taps into that ancient wisdom."

THE CHURCH IN THE CITY: *Imagine Garfield Heights*

Everyone in Garfield Heights, Ohio, is proud of their public high-school students for leading a community visioning process in this blue-collar suburb of Cleveland. The Diocese of Cleveland became the catalyst for this remarkable expression of the power of positive imaging when it offered Appreciative Inquiry consultation to community leaders as part of "The Church in the City," an initiative of Bishop Anthony Pilla that is designed to reinvigorate central cities through new forms of partnership and redevelopment.

Garfield Heights' school superintendent Ronald L. Victor credits the Appreciative Inquiry process with demonstrating "the incredible capacity kids have to do things to build up the whole community." The transformation began in 1998 when Superintendent Victor heard Rick Krivanka talk about Imagine Chicago, a community-growth initiative created by AI pioneer and Episcopal priest Bliss Browne.[5] It was the first process to use young people as interviewers and has been widely replicated in communities around the world. Krivanka was able to help Victor adapt the program to Garfield Heights. The public high-school students from Garfield Heights and students from Trinity Catholic High School were given the opportunity to participate as consultants to the town. "This is what consultants do," Victor told them. "They go out and survey people, analyze the data, and report back on what they found." The students were eager to volunteer, and in 1999 they began Imagine Garfield Heights.

Using questions adapted from those used in Imagine Chicago, a team of students from the two high schools interviewed a cross-section of community leaders about what gives life to the city and what could be done to enhance its future. Here is a summary of the questions they used in the Discovery process:

• How long have you lived in Garfield Heights? In this community? What first brought your family here? What's it like for you to live in this community?

• When you think about the whole city of Garfield Heights, are there particular places or people or images that represent the city to you?

• Thinking back over your Garfield Heights memories, what have been real high points for you as a citizen of this city — times when you felt most alive, proud, excited about being a part of this community?

• Why did these experiences mean so much to you?

• How would you describe the quality of life in Garfield Heights today?

• What changes in the city would you most like to see? What do you imagine your own role might be in helping to make this happen? Who could work with you?

• Close your eyes and imagine Garfield Heights, as you most want it to be a generation from now. What is it like? What do you see and hear? What are you proudest of having accomplished?

• As you think back over this conversation, what images stand out for you as capturing your hopes for this city's future?

• What do you think would be an effective process for getting people across the city talking and working together on behalf of Garfield Heights' future? Whom would you want to draw into a Garfield Heights conversation?

Each time the students reported their findings it was to a larger and more appreciative audience — first at a joint city council and school board meeting of 250 people, and later at an ecumenical prayer service of 400 people. In the second phase in 2000, a larger team from Garfield Heights High

School expanded their interviews citywide to include informal community leaders and residents. They subsequently made presentations before the wider community.

In August 2001 a community leadership conference brought together more than 75 community leaders and members of Imagine Garfield Heights. From this leadership conference and data gathered by Imagine Garfield Heights emerged six specific objectives for the city: visionary leadership, excellent schools, all-inclusive recreation, attractive retail, outstanding cooperation, and quality housing. In direct response to these objectives, the Garfield Heights City Schools developed a new mission statement reflecting these objectives and the creative perspective that is a part of the AI philosophy:

"The Garfield Heights Learning Community demonstrates basic values that meet the needs of the heart with clear academic goals applying to all children in appropriate facilities and where all community members work together."

RESULTS

With the momentum from the interviews, the school system began producing a community-wide newsletter in response to requests from people in the community. In November 2000 the community supported a 41.5 million-dollar bond issue for a new high-school complex and other additions and renovations for district facilities, and it passed on the first try. The new high school, including a performing-arts center and a community-health and physical-education center reflects the visions of the people that public schools should serve the whole community. The state responded to the obvious enthusiasm of residents and qualified the district's Master Plan for additional funds. That may provide the district with up to $19 million to complete the 10-year $84 million building project. As an added benefit, proficiency scores of high-school students have shown continuous improvement since Imagine Garfield Heights began. With the help of alternative programs, few students have been suspended or expelled.

In the third phase of the project every single student in the public high school participated in an interview with another student about the quality of life within the school. The students presented the information to more than 400 teachers, administrators and support staff in a district-wide gathering. The students arrived at positive and workable suggestions, and the adults listened. Following this meeting a high-school senior on the student team said, "A number of high-school teachers came up to me afterward and said they never realized how much students cared about the things we reported. These teachers said that they will really go out of their way to do things that mean so much to students." The student also noted that a staff member at an elementary school in the district said that teachers discussed afterward how they could adapt the ideas from the high school for younger students. Influencing the teachers in a positive way, promoting understanding of the students' thinking, and motivating the teachers to act did not come through directives. The shift came through a process of asking questions about what students really appreciated and cared about, and then openly sharing examples of what was said.[6] A change initiative spearheaded by youth, Imagine Garfield Heights brings to mind Isaiah (11:6), *"and a little child shall lead them."*

THE DIOCESE OF CLEVELAND: VIBRANT PARISH LIFE

In his 2001 pastoral letter entitled "Vibrant Parish Life," Bishop Anthony M. Pilla of the Diocese of Cleveland wrote, "I see parish life as so central to our diocesan well-being that I would say, 'As the parish goes, so goes the faith of the people.' If the Church is to flourish in the 21st century, we must offer, maintain, and support a vibrant parish life for every Catholic." In this letter Bishop Pilla offers "four convictions" for this work:

• "Our chosen method for achieving vibrant parish life for all of our people must be an experience of 'communion'— growing together in Christ.

• Any solutions we develop must come from and be embraced willingly with the heart by the local communities involved. I respect and rely upon the leadership of those closest to the situation. I do not believe that true parish life can be imposed from an outside authority figure ... Building vibrant parish life ... demands local leadership.

• The priests, deacons, religious and lay ecclesiastical ministers serving the parishes of our diocese must be respected and their faithful cooperation is essential.

• Vibrant parish life is best achieved through the collaborative efforts of several ministries and communities in an area, and these ministries will often permeate parish boundaries."

Rick Krivanka of the Diocese of Cleveland Pastoral Planning Office notes that the name and scope of this letter reflects Appreciative Inquiry principles in addressing parish realities with hopeful and compelling images in contrast to framing the situation as a set of problems. Based on the Gospel, they also clearly reflect the appreciative design processes of strong social bonding, full inclusion of all stakeholders, homegrown control wherever feasible, and cooperation across boundaries.

To discover the strengths of the diocese, Bishop Pilla asked each of Cleveland's 235 parishes to undergo a self-study, looking at their "gifts, vibrancy, and needs." Parishioners could gather data about their parish through several methods, including appreciative interviews. The interview questions assessed parish strengths in various categories: beginning moments, celebrating the Eucharist, teaching, caring, evangelizing, participating, and visioning. Here is a sample of the questions:

• When you are feeling best about your membership in our parish today, what image of parish life comes to mind?

• What is the single most important thing our parish has contributed to your life?

• Describe what is most nourishing and life-giving about our celebration of the Eucharist.

• What can you envision our parish doing in the next two to three years to call you and our people to an even fuller experience of the Eucharist?

• Think of a time when you participated in an educational or spiritual growth opportunity at our parish that really made a difference in your relationship with God. Tell the story of this experience.

• How can we improve our efforts to provide Catholic education and faith development in ways that would really help our faith become more alive and a part of daily life for you and your family?

• What do you see in our parish outreach efforts that have been of real service to people, and an inspiration to you? How can we more fully be of service to the neighborhood and broader community, particularly in partnership with others (other parishes, faith communities, community groups, etc.)? What exciting possibilities can you envision?

• When have you felt most welcomed and included at our parish? What in particular did people say or do that made you feel welcomed and included? How can our parish be much more welcoming to parishioners, to inactive parishioners or visitors?

• Think of a time when you participated in a worthwhile educational, spiritual, or social opportunity at a neighboring parish. What was the activity and where did it take place? What in particular did you most appreciate about this activity? What could we do to foster greater cooperation between neighboring parishes?

• In your opinion, what are the two to three best resources and greatest examples of vibrancy in our parish?

• If you could imagine or transform our parish in any way you wished, what one to three things would you do to enhance its life and vitality? Can you envision any of the three wishes you have described being done cooperatively with another parish? Which programs or ministries? Which neighboring parishes?

Because parishes in the United States have typically seen themselves as well-defined entities answerable to their diocese and the bishop, but only peripherally related to other parishes, Bishop Pilla asked that the self-study lead to work with neighboring parishes on avenues for cooperation and sharing. He wanted to exchange that "congregational perspective" for a Catholic perspective, to see the diocese as the basic unit of the Church with all local faith communities in communion with one another. To Pilla, this can and should be done, and appreciative approaches help move in that direction. When parishes link in an appreciative way with one another, they are better able to serve the needs of the surrounding community. As Pilla notes, these linked parishes can in turn link with other faith communities, "serving the common good and celebrating our shared heritage as children of God."

RESULTS

Appreciative Inquiry motivates parishioners toward greater faith, unity and assumption of personal responsibility. Diocese Pastoral Planning Office member Gail Roussey has seen it happen. She says, "at the basis of the vision of Vibrant Parish Life is the idea that the laypeople have to own their role in the church, — and they have to begin to really participate in setting directions and become the church in a deeper way than they have in the past. That's what these listening processes do for people. They come to realize how much faith they have. It's not just the faith that the institution has but also the faith they hold." Roussey's colleague David DeLambo agrees, saying, "The power is in the reading of the comments. It's an evangelization moment when they read what their fellow parishioners have to say. That's where the Good News of God's presence in the parish is reported to them. It's the parish's own Gospel. They have to read their own Gospel in order to be evangelized by it."

Longtime church activist Lou Keim participated in Appreciative Inquiry at St. Malachi Parish and the Community of St. Malachi. She also feels that if AI continues in the Church it will reinforce greater lay participation. She believes that AI "binds the group together" and energizes participants so much that they take their excitement into their workplaces and to everyone they know. In Keim's estimation, that's good public relations, "another plus for the Catholic Church."

One pastor involved in the self-study declared that Appreciative Inquiry is "validated time and time again. You always wonder how you can get more than just one or two opinions when you're making a decision. And this is the structure or the way that can happen. People who did participate probably felt a strong sense of ownership of the goals that were set and the mission of our parish. We used two phrases: 'Who we are and what we stand for.' We used this process to keep moving in the right direction and are doing it in an extremely positive way."

That positive energy inspires Krivanka. As he listens and participates in Appreciative Inquiries that highlight and draw on the best of parish life, he says he feels deeply impressed by the faith and the commitment of people. "I sit there and think, this is my job, and this is my work, to be with people like this. I tell people, 'If you saw what I saw, you would be so proud of being Catholic.'"

CHAPTER 4

PLANNING

Using Appreciative Inquiry

for Strategic Planning and

Creating Mission Statements

PLANNING

Using Appreciative Inquiry for Strategic Planning and Creating Mission Statements

A NATIONWIDE DIALOGUE ON CATHOLIC HEALTH CARE IN CANADA

 Catholics who serve as healers and caregivers in health care organizations are familiar with the challenges care providers face in days when budgets can barely keep pace with people's needs. The Catholic Health Association of Canada (CHAC)[1] saw that all types of Catholic health ministries faced both challenge and opportunity. According to CHAC President Richard Haughian, "We felt that the ministry was at a turning point [and] a visioning process had-n't been done since the early 90s. The question was how to make it as inclu-sive as possible. AI, with its emphasis on stories, beginning with your strengths and building on them, and involving as many people as possible in the process, was very appealing to us." In collaboration with the Canadian Conference of Catholic Bishops (CCCB), member provincial health associa-tions, sponsor organizations, and other interested parties, the CHAC chose to sponsor a nationwide dialogue on a preferred future for the Catholic health ministry in Canada.

The CHAC formed a Steering Committee and in September 2002 the CHAC board and the committee met in a two-day retreat with their AI consultant, Jacqueline Pelletier. They were introduced to the Appreciative Inquiry process and from that formulated these five major topics and ques-tions for the National Dialogue.

NATIONAL DIALOGUE QUESTIONNAIRE EXCERPTS

PREAMBLE

There are many ways that we are engaged in the Catholic health ministry—as care providers in hospitals, chronic and long-term care institu-tions; as workers in social service agencies and centers; as caregivers in parishes, in community groups, at home with our loved ones. Together we form a vast community of people dedicated to the service of others.

TOPIC 1: CONTINUING THE HEALING MINISTRY

Each day we see people who demonstrate dedication, perseverance and devotion in the compassionate care they provide. Such persons radiate commitment and enthusiasm. The Catholic health and healing ministry, rooted in Gospel values, is at its best when it strives to free people from physical and spiritual suffering, enabling them to live more fully.

• Share a significant experience you have had in the healing ministry, or that you are aware of, that enabled someone to live more fully.

• What made this experience possible? What was it about you, the other people, the organization, the situation, etc. that contributed?

TOPIC 2: DARING TO MEET UNMET NEEDS

Throughout the history of our country, women and men of deep faith have responded to unmet health and social needs. These pioneers shaped the future of the Catholic health ministry and of health and social services in Canada. We remember their daring, creativity and determination. Moved by the needs of their day, they planned wisely, trusted in God, and acted with confidence and hope.

• Tell me a story about someone who inspired you by their daring, trust or creativity in the healing ministry.

• Share about a time when you, or your organization, lived the same spirit.

• What made that experience possible? What was it about you, the people with you, the organization, the situation, etc that contributed?

TOPIC 3: ATTENTIVENESS TO THE WHOLE PERSON

We all have physical, social and spiritual needs that require attention. Healing takes into account the wholeness of the person, recognizing the interrelationship of body, mind, and spirit. Such an understanding of healing affirms the dignity of persons and recognizes that healing is more than simply curing disease. It can mean restoring confidence and pride, providing a sense of community, or helping someone to forgive. Those of us engaged in the Catholic health ministry strive to nurture health and healing by providing compassionate and holistic care.

• Tell me a story or share an experience when you gave or witnessed such attentiveness.

• What enabled that experience to happen? What was it about you, the other people with you, the organization, the situation, etc. that contributed?

TOPIC 4: THE PROMOTION OF JUSTICE

The Christian tradition views healthy relationships, the protection of individual human rights, and the common good as basic to a healthy, peaceful and just society. It emphasizes the link between promoting health and working to overcome injustice. The vision of the Catholic health ministry seeks not only to respond to sickness and suffering, but also to counter the causes of injustice.
• Share an experience you had or witnessed that exemplifies justice being lived in the Catholic health ministry.
• What enabled that experience to happen? What was it about you, the other people with you, the organization, the situation that contributed, etc?

TOPIC 5: ACTING ON OUR STRENGTHS

Engaging and envisioning provides an opportunity to go beyond what we thought was possible. It is time to push the creative edges of possibility and to wonder about the ministry's greatest potential.
• You have identified some unique strengths that characterize the ministry. How do you think we could best act on these strengths as individuals, organizations and parish communities?
• What are your 3 wishes that would make the Catholic health ministry even more exceptional and unique?[2]

The goal of the National Dialogue was to include not only all members of the Catholic Health Association of Canada, but also representatives from Catholic Social Services, dioceses and parishes, patients, residents and clients of Catholic health institutions, the Catholic Women's League, the Knights of Columbus, and other interested organizations and individuals. A bilingual Facilitators Guide (available on the CHAC website) allowed interviewers across Canada to participate in gathering data autonomously. Interviewers were given freedom to choose interviewees from their organization, parish and community for the 30 to 60 minute interviews. About 53% of respondents were associated with Catholic health care organizations and 47% were from other Catholic organizations and settings. Over 1500 interviews were completed in seven months and the findings were grouped under four themes: "We believe, we hope, we can do better, and we suggest the following actions."

Sandra Keon[3] facilitated dialogues in her hospital and coordinated dialogues for her Diocese. She admitted, "The process was new to us, but when it was first introduced, we felt that it fit very well with the ministry—an inclusive and transparent process is exactly what we were looking for and we wanted to do a broad consultation. As a facilitator, it provided participants with the opportunity to dialogue about the ministry's strengths. For the Diocese, we structured it around a one-hour process. We brought together a group of 15-20 people — parishioners, priests, etc. who broke out into dialogues. Everyone was really excited to talk. They didn't feel inhibited. It was an energy-generating process. There were a lot of statements that were high moments for me."

RESULTS

The data was gathered for "A National Forum" in Montreal in May 2003. At the Forum, about 360 participants reviewed the findings and participated in a visioning process. They developed Provocative Propositions based on the data. The small groups were energized and one participant said, "People were inspired to speak from the heart and to be courageous in their remarks. There was a lot of risk-taking happening." Last, the convention divided into provincial/regional groups to work on action plans for their particular sector.

Sister Patricia Cuddihy[4] was very strongly influenced by her introduction to AI at the conference. She and the other sisters of her congregation, the Religious Hospitallers of St. Joseph, will be going through a major transformation in the next year because they have given up their role in managing a major health organization. She indicated that the results of the National Dialogue would strongly influence their future directions. Sr. Cuddihy said, "After yesterday morning's workshop on Appreciative Inquiry, I'll never look at the negative again in the same way."

ARCHDIOCESE OF LOS ANGELES: *Pastoral Council Office*

Vatican II and Canon Law recommend establishing parish pastoral councils, with lay members selected to serve in a consultative role to the pastor on practical action-oriented matters. Before major personnel cuts in 2002, Maria Elena Uribe was the Pastoral Council's Office Coordinator for the Archdiocese of Los Angeles, a sprawling complex of 286 Catholic parishes. When she first began to help parish councils to plan, Uribe picked up on their feelings of distress. The demands of their roles and the tedious nature of most strategic planning can overwhelm council members. After learning about Appreciative Inquiry at an annual meeting on council planning, Uribe saw a perfect context for everything she had wanted to accomplish, and a longed-for renewal of parish life felt within reach.

Since most councils are expected to go through yearly spiritual formation, Uribe offered one- to three-day spiritually based workshops to develop a shared vision and deep commitments. Sometimes several pastoral councils shared the expense of a consultant in one Appreciative Inquiry workshop. The individual teams worked on their own church issues but had the advantage of cross-fertilization from the other parish councils. The appreciative approach — finding what works instead of focusing on problems — encouraged not just attendance but also openness. Pastors appeared to visibly relax as the council told them what was working in their parishes. Pastors could then more readily accept that parish council members were really supportive and helpful "experts" on parish life. As one pastor said, "I found out positive things I never knew before."

What could be more consistent with Catholicism than a process that results in rebirth? Reflecting on the increased satisfaction in her own work since using Appreciative Inquiry, Uribe beamed: "I can understand how Jesus felt when Lazarus woke up."

DIOCESE OF OAKLAND: *Youth Ministry Report*

Mark Fischer of the Diocese of Oakland Pastoral Council recalled his awakening to Appreciative Inquiry in a 1997 article in *Today's Parish*[5]. In a meeting led by Most Reverend John S. Cummins, Bishop of the Diocese of Oakland, CA. Fischer and other members of the Pastoral Council were looking at ways to assess a draft report on youth ministry. Bishop Cummins opened the meeting with a reading of the prophecy of Joel (2:28): *"Then afterward I will pour out my spirit on all flesh, your sons and your daughters shall prophesy, your old men shall dream dreams, and your young men shall see visions."* He then continued with a prayer that revolved around appreciative questions and became an inspired inquiry and reflection of more than an hour.

"Bishop Cummins invited the 20 council members to recall their own memories of the Church when they were young, and then to express how they felt that God's Spirit was 'speaking' through the Youth Ministry Report," Fischer wrote. What followed was "an extraordinary outpouring of memory, self-revelation, anecdote, appreciation of the subcommittee, critique, and discernment," Fischer says. "By the end of the prayer we had not only 'prayed' but also accomplished the most important part of our 'work' regarding the report."

DIOCESE OF CLEVELAND: *Pastoral Planning Office*

Several years ago the staff of the Pastoral Planning Office at the Diocese of Cleveland became familiar with Appreciative Inquiry, but it wasn't the primary methodology for parish pastoral planning. After attending a three-day workshop with AI theorist David Cooperrider at Case Western Reserve University, staff members Rick Krivanka, David DeLambo, and Gail Roussey shelved their previous strategic planning guidelines and focused instead on developing and fully integrating AI into all the work of the Pastoral Planning Office.

DeLambo explains the shift with a story that underscores both the traps of traditional planning and his faith in Appreciative Inquiry as a preferred alternative. One day he was conducting a planning retreat for a local parish staff and pastoral council. While using a basic SWOT analysis (strengths, weaknesses, opportunities, threats), DeLambo noticed that "Folks spent about 15 minutes listing the parish strengths, and over an hour listing its weaknesses." The group managed to put together positive goals to work on in the coming year, but they were clearly not feeling good about what they accomplished. As he was leaving, a distressed woman approached him. "There is so much that needed addressing," she said, "and I feel worse about the parish now than when we started." DeLambo continues, "Her comment really stayed with me. I remember thinking that there was something inherently wrong with this approach to planning. These folks should have been coming out of this planning process feeling empowered, with a blueprint in hand to make a positive change in their parish, but they weren't. They had a plan, but lacked the energy, excitement, and enthusiasm necessary to make the plan work." DeLambo felt especially sorry for the pastor and staff. "They spent an afternoon listening to parish leaders weigh in on deficiencies in the parish, and in some cases, deficiencies in their ministry. Pastors often tell me that for every one letter complimenting the ministry of the parish, they receive ten criticizing it. This planning process was more of the same for the parish staff. My skin certainly isn't thick enough to handle that kind of constant criticism. That day I saw why pastoral staffs don't always embrace planning. And I couldn't blame them!"

RESULTS

Since the Diocese of Cleveland Pastoral Planning Office began to use Appreciative Inquiry, there has been much more demand for strategic-planning consultation. Today, their consultations often begin by administering a preliminary set of questions to parish leaders. This initial set of general interviews serves to provide the information necessary to formulate specific high-priority topics and questions to be used in the larger set of interviews with the wider parish. Following are results in two specific parishes of the Diocese, St. Christopher and St. Mary.

ST. CHRISTOPHER PARISH: *Mission Statement and Guiding Values*

In consultation with the Diocese of Cleveland Pastoral Planning Office, St. Christopher Parish in Rocky River, Ohio, used Appreciative Inquiry to create a parish mission statement and a set of guiding values. To begin the process, Fr. John Chlebo, Pastor of St. Christopher, convened a meeting of the parish leaders. After an introduction and 15 minutes of prayer, appreciative questions focused on two key topics:

• *Stories of Faith and Life:* Describe an experience at St. Christopher Parish when you felt most alive, most fulfilled, or most enthused about your parish. Share the story of this 'best moment.' What made it the best moment? Who were the significant others involved and why were they significant?"

Participants were asked first to reflect silently on the questions, and then to share their responses, one at a time, in small groups. Everyone was asked to listen to each response without discussion. All responses were then recorded on flip charts.

• *Our Core Values:* Based on these shared Stories of Faith and Life, what values best express who we are and what we stand for as a parish community?"

All participants were again asked to reflect silently on the question, and then to share their personal responses one by one. All responses were recorded on flip charts. Each group was then instructed to pick the top five responses. The entire group then reconvened to listen to all of the responses and to create a mission statement from them. The mission statement that emerged was simple and expressive:

"We are the people of St. Christopher Catholic Church, a spirited community of faith dedicated to welcome, celebrate, care, and grow in the image and likeness of Jesus."

The mission statement was presented to the entire parish for input and approval, and celebrated publicly. Next, based on the core values embodied in the mission statement — Welcome, Celebrate, Care, and Grow — a second set of appreciative questions was developed. This interview protocol stated each core value, followed by a short descriptive paragraph and two appreciative questions. Here, for example, is how "Welcome" read in the second interview:

Welcome:

"As a parish, we value being a warm and welcoming community. We want to welcome all people — different people with different gifts — to fully participate in our worship, teaching, service, and ministry.

• Describe a time when you felt that we truly conveyed an inviting and welcoming community to people. What do we do best to welcome people to participate?

• As you look to the future, what can we do to really encourage more people to feel welcome and participate in parish life?"

Based on the results of these interviews with parishioners, a set of goals for parish life was developed. Under the value of "Welcome," for example, the following five themes were developed:

1. "Communicate parish activities in ways that better reach people.
2. Develop more ways to welcome and involve parishioners.
3. Enhance our welcoming spirit at Mass.
4. Encourage parish involvement through personal invitation.
5. Recognize and welcome individuals of all ages."

The parish community tested the themes using a paper-and-pencil consensus validation survey. For each theme, parishioners rated two things: "How important is this to you?" and "How well is this now done in our parish?"

RESULTS

Fr. Chlebo says that the overriding goal that emerged in the appreciative planning process was to enhance parish communication. "We now have a parish newsletter for the first time which has already grown to eight pages," he says. "In our building campaign, we weren't just trying to build a church; we were trying to build a community." As a result of the consultation, Fr. Chlebo says, "Overall there is a more positive feeling at St. Chris and people are friendlier to each other."

ST. MARY PARISH: *Pastoral Planning*

Fr. Stephen Vellenga, Pastor of St. Mary Parish in Painesville, Ohio, encouraged his parish to use Appreciative Inquiry for pastoral planning. St. Mary's is a widely diverse parish with urban, suburban, and rural territory that in the last 10 years has incorporated a large Hispanic community. As a new pastor there, Fr. Vellenga realized that the community was looking for spiritual leadership that would free people. He felt that the AI process would facilitate this type of leadership dynamic.

Fr. Vellenga readily accepted the idea that a pastoral council's job was pastoral planning. "In the past, people often didn't do planning," he says. "We just said, 'Well, it's always been done this way so that's the way we'll do it now.' In the Catholic Church, over the last 25 years we've gotten the idea that we can plan, develop a vision, and achieve a desired outcome. The three-year involvement of St. Mary's laity with Appreciative Inquiry planning brought about a sense of pride and ownership."

RESULTS

St. Mary Parish Council President Mary Pat Frey worked with the Diocese of Cleveland Pastoral Planning Office and Fr. Vellenga to train parish leaders in the Appreciative Inquiry process. Although they had not yet finished the formal goal setting, Frey sensed a definite momentum. "It's neat to see how things have started to happen. People already doing ministries are even more active — they were affirmed in the AI process." On the flip side, the process also revealed obvious challenges. Frey sees positive movement toward addressing those issues, in part because of Fr. Vellenga's encouragement to follow through on good ideas. "If you have a great idea, go ahead and do it," he says. For instance, a wish for greeters emerged in the interviews. "Now we have greeters in the church," Frey says. "We haven't yet set these goals but changes have started to happen because the information is out there. We're already challenged by it, we're affirmed by it, and shining more brightly because of it. Those things are just happening because it's been called to our attention and we've taken small but visible steps."

BENEDICTINE UNIVERSITY

Benedictine University is a mission of the Benedictine monks of St. Procopius Abbey. With the facilitation of Dr. James Ludema, associate professor of Organization Development, the university used Appreciative Inquiry to reaffirm and advance its Benedictine identity. In contrast to traditional values clarification processes, the AI approach included a broad cross-section of the Benedictine community. It centered on establishing a clear and compelling Benedictine University identity based on a common vision embraced in practice. It was part of a two-year strategic planning process launched by Provost Mary Daly Lewis and by Assistant to the Provost for Institutional Mission, Fr. David Turner.

Appreciative values clarification finds the core identity of the organization and empowers people to act from that "inspirational ideal." It has several characteristics:
- It starts with the mission and identifies core values and principles.
- It expresses the walk as well as the talk of the organization.
- It encourages every employee to strive to reflect the values in his or her work.

Six core values that reflect the Benedictine heritage were reaffirmed and advanced as a result of the process:

- A search for God by oneself and with others
- A tradition of hospitality
- An appreciation for living and working in community
- A concern for the development of each person
- An emphasis on life lived in balance
- A dedication to responsible stewardship of the earth

RESULTS

Dr. Ludema points out that the Benedictine values already existed as a positive core, but the Appreciative Inquiry process helped "reinforce and bring them to life." The process included interviews with students, faculty, staff, administration, parents and other constituents, and a university-wide Benedictine identity retreat using AI. The AI process advanced the Benedictine identity in a number of ways. First, it provided participants with a renewed sense of connection to the history of Benedictine University. Second, it provided an opportunity for people to establish new relationships and to strengthen the sense of community on campus. Third, it allowed participants to reconnect with the University's core strengths and values. Finally, it led to a series of specific action initiatives including:

1. A series of "user-friendly" readers on Catholic and Benedictine identity written by Fr. David Turner.
2. A new orientation program for students, faculty and staff.
3. A colorful brochure on the University's Benedictine identity to be used for external communications and promotions.
4. A Benedictine identity video entitled "The Benedictine Difference" that demonstrates the expression of the Benedictine values in the life of the University.
5. Plans for a National Heritage in Action Conference for Benedictine High Schools to be held at Benedictine University.

The goal was to weave the core values into the "organizational DNA" and according to Fr. David Turner, the two-year Appreciative Inquiry process did just that.

CARMELITE BROTHERS: *A New Mantle for a New Millennium*

Bro. Larry Fidelus, O.Carm. was introduced to Appreciative Inquiry at Benedictine University, where his Ph.D. thesis was "The Transformational Potential of the Powerful Positive Question." For Bro. Fidelus, "there is a spiritual journey around powerful questions." He notes that AI is both a philosophy and a methodology, but he wonders if we need always tie the philosophy to the specific discovery-dream-design-delivery methodology. Many other AI practitioners also sense that the methodology will continue to evolve as we all gain more experience.

When the Carmelite Brothers of the Province of the Most Pure Heart of Mary had their tri-annual gathering in 1999 they chose a process with appreciative questions woven throughout five days of meetings. The 200 brothers came from the United States, Canada, Mexico, and Peru, a diverse group of men representing different ministries. With a newly elected slate of leaders and a new millennium on the horizon, they wanted to explore three topics: Community (how we live together), Ministry (how we serve together), and Identity (how we are seen together).

Their goal was to create "A New Mantle for a New Millennium"— a shared vision of a "lived Carmelite experience in the 21st century." The group did only the "discover" and "dream" steps, but according to the positive evaluations, they derived great benefit. The men broke into small groups balanced for diversity, each at a table with a trained facilitator. They discussed community, ministry, and identity in separate sessions in common format:

• Open with candle lighting and prayer.

• Read a relevant story.

• Share a peak experience related to the topic one at a time. Examples from the topic areas include "Describe a time when you had an extraordinarily deep sense of community." "Describe a time when your ministry was most energizing and enlivening." "Name and describe a practice, idea, or symbol that most clearly images or defines 'us' in your mind and heart."

• Explore "What do these experiences have in common?" — or "What are the key characteristics of the experiences that have just been related?"

• Explore "What do we learn from these experiences?"

• Imagine/dream "How do we create environments in which moments of deep community can happen again and again?" "What ministries will generate similar moments of energy and life in the future?" "What will be the practices, ideas, or symbols that will most clearly image 'us' in the future?"

• Visualize, based on what we've learned so far, "What will we be like in regard to community, ministry, and identity in the years to come?"

RESULTS

The evaluations were terrific. Comments included "an act of sheer genius," "excellent," "superb," "showed respect for the wisdom of our brothers," "Wrestling with real issues in an affirming and fun experience made this the best. Let's keep doing this. I got a sense of hope from it all."[6]

VINCENTIANS CENTRAL HOUSE COMMUNITY: *Annual Planning*

The various local communities of Vincentians (Congregation of the Mission) in the Philippines have adopted Appreciative Inquiry as a method for doing their annual planning. One of these communities is the Central House community, a group of twelve members engaged in ministries such as education, parish work, Marian devotion, and human development. This community is always stretched for time; the members usually come together only for prayers in the morning, meals, and a brief get-together at the end of the day. They agreed to meet for three hours every evening over the course of three days to come up with an annual plan. They began with these discovery questions.
1. Think of a time (a "peak experience") when you really felt most alive, most excited and most committed as a member of your local Vincentian community. What and when was that experience or incident? Why was it a "peak experience" for you? What role did you play in it? Who was with you?
2. What do you value most about: Yourself; Your membership in the Congregation; Your present ministry/work/assignment?
3. Take a bird's eye view of your local community. What do you think are your unique strengths as a community? What gives life to your community?
4. Imagine your community five years from today. You have just been voted by the entire Congregation to be the "best" local community in the world. How did you deserve this title? What is your vision for your community? What is happening in your community that best expresses your deepest aspirations and dreams? State three wishes you have for your community that would build on your existing strengths.

Fr. Banaga, the facilitator of the process, finds Appreciative Inquiry highly suited to his Asian culture because it is a "very gentle" process. In contrast to Westerners, who are sometimes perceived to be confrontational and aggressive, Asians are much more polite and sensitive to the feelings of others. In working toward change and improvement, Asians sometimes "coat" their language to avoid offending or blaming others or putting them down. In a similar way, AI looks at the strengths of people and builds on them rather than tearing people apart with criticism. Because of that cultural compatibility and the success of their first experience with AI in their annual planning, the Vincentians plan to use the process on a continual basis.

SPRINGFIELD DOMINICANS: *Parable Conference*

Several orders of religious women are beginning to use Appreciative Inquiry for planning and development, as well as for spiritual retreats. In their lives of constant giving, the nurturing and life-enhancing nature of AI is a perfect approach, as some Dominican sisters have discovered.

St. Dominic, founder of the Order of Preachers in the 13th century, developed a reflective learning organization that was participatory and democratic. This Dominican order valued women and men, clergy and lay, and was alive with emotional passion for the Gospel. St. Dominic believed in the importance of conversation with God and about God as the foundation for an ongoing search for truth. As one commentator said, "Eloquence is the sound which a passionate soul makes. So Dominic had no need to found schools of rhetoric in order to send preachers into the world; all he needed was to touch the heart of his age and to find there or awaken there a passion."[7]

Sr. Marilyn Jean Runkel, O.P., whose Ph.D. thesis at Benedictine University was on the impact of St. Dominic on Catholic education, calls him "a revolutionary for his time" and takes his call to participatory democracy to heart. She has used Appreciative Inquiry to do planning with her own religious community, the Springfield Dominicans.

Within Dominican democracy each congregation is independent. The separate congregations work collaboratively on social-justice issues and participate in projects that foster the process of sharing resources and knowledge. The Parable Conference for Dominican Life and Mission provides spiritual retreats, study tours, and preaching teams. Sr. Runkel led the staff of Parable in a day of appreciative reflection and goal planning. Her Discovery questions included the following:

• What positive impact have the goals of Parable had on you personally?
• How has Parable impacted Dominican Life within the order?
• What about the work of Parable do we want to carry into the future?
• What are areas around which we need creativity, new ways of meeting needs?
• What will Parable look like in 2010?

The Discovery process, and the planning that followed, produced high marks from the staff. They found that Appreciative Inquiry produced so many quality creative ideas they had "enough to do for 40 years." That doesn't surprise Runkel. "From the beginning I thought AI was connected to the way we should do planning in the Church — looking to the positive and facilitating based on what's right," she says. Runkel finds that this more participative process, as encouraged by Vatican II, produces the best planning. Dominic himself involved his whole religious community in governance, and that governance is bound to be "very democratic and kind of messy." Runkel's hope is that the leaders of the Church can learn to tolerate the ambiguity inherent in a creative process such as AI, pointing out that modern chaos theory[8] backs up her call for patience: "Chaos brings creativity if we can be open to the chaos long enough."

SISTERS OF NOTRE DAME[9]: *National Collaboration*

In 2002, the four provinces of the Sisters of Notre Dame (Coesfeld[10]) began a national collaborative effort using Appreciative Inquiry. "We were responding to an invitation from our Superior General in Rome, Sr. Mary Sujita Kallupurakkathu, to address 'How might we listen in order to learn and to search together in responding to our call to mission today?'" says Chardon, Ohio Province's Sr. Lisa Novak. "We wanted to get broad participation from our sisters in the US provinces from the beginning. After much discussion in our national committee, we chose to use the AI process and follow where it would lead us in our ongoing formation for mission."

Sr. Novak and Sr. Jacquelyn Gusdane worked with Rick Krivanka from the Diocese of Cleveland and representatives from four provinces to create an initial interview process for use with the provincial leaders. These leaders discerned and developed topics which evolved into five life-giving images. Sisters Novak and Gusdane then designed an interview protocol for use with the sisters across the country. More than 600 interviews were conducted in the fall of 2002. Each interviewer submitted the outcome of her interview into an overall summary for each province with the help of an internet tool developed by the Diocese and Brulant, a local IT consulting firm.

The interviews proved significant. According to Sr. Shauna Bankemper, coordinator of the national Formation for Mission Committee, "So much energy is being created — and this is important. The interviews are powerful and energizing. If we did nothing else, the interviews alone were worth it."

In each province, discernment teams were formed around the life-giving images and hopes and dreams of the membership. Their mandate was to read, pray over, listen for and then identify the key themes in the members' interview responses. An interprovince newsletter highlighted and supported each life-giving image with best quotes, phrases and images. The images included:

- Engaging in Relational Living: Women marked by warmth, welcome, and caring
- Choosing Community: Women bound together in Jesus' name and service
- Deepening and Sharing Our Spirituality: Spiritual and wholesome women of God
- Partnering in the Mission of Jesus: Women on fire for mission
- Experiencing Internationality/Embracing Diversity: Women with hearts as wide as the world.

RESULTS

In July 2003, a national gathering was held at the invitation of Sr. Kallupurakkathu and 575 sisters attended "to reflect on our mission and ministry experiences and consider new possibilities and priorities for incarnating the Congregation's charism and spirit in today's Church and world." Sr. Gusdane says that the response to the overall process and the gathering "far exceeded our dreams. Often I sit back and marvel at what the AI process has generated among us. We have affirmed our past and present by naming our best moments. Now we embrace the future fully aware of our potential to create new realities by our life-giving choices."

CHAPTER 5

PASSAGES

Using Appreciative Inquiry

to Enhance

Transitions

PASSAGES

Using Appreciative Inquiry to Enhance Transitions

A CHANGE OF PASTOR

Transitions are opportunities for transformation. Appreciative Inquiry can increase wisdom during times of change. For example, one of the most challenging times for a parish is the transition from one pastor to another. The Church has a few structures to help the clergy, but the community may be lost in the shuffle. People develop close bonds with their pastor and when a pastor moves, the congregation is often still grieving when the new pastor arrives. At St. Francis Xavier parish in Gettysburg, Pennsylvania, the new pastor, Fr. Bernardo Pistone, had to be honest about the challenge. "I've spent 20 of my 27 years in the priesthood at St. Mary's in Lancaster," he announced. "I'm sad. Give me time." His difficulty letting go was matched by those of his former parishioners, who even months later arrived at Gettysburg wearing T-shirts bearing his photo and the caption "Fr. Pistone Fan Club."

Healing is a journey through feelings of loss, but the transition to hope is easier when we use Appreciative Inquiry. Maria Elena Uribe, of the Archdiocese of Los Angeles, favors getting the whole parish community involved in the process of saying goodbye and hello simultaneously by looking back on peak experiences. By asking appreciative questions, parishioners can better survive the transition and grow from the experience. The entire parish can be interviewed, or the parish may form a smaller transition team to manage the inquiry and the information from the interviews. Here are some sample questions for this type of inquiry:

• What are the qualities you value most in our outgoing pastor? In what ways has he helped you to embody those qualities in your own life?

• What do you value the most about our parish?

• What do you most want our new pastor to know about our parish?

• What are the three concrete wishes you have for our parish's future?

The team can use the stories about the outgoing pastor to prepare a heartfelt goodbye for him, but the interviews also gather data to let the new pastor know what the parish values most. The team may also find out how the new pastor would like to be welcomed by asking, "When you have felt welcomed before, what happened?" They may post the answers, along with a photo and biography of the incoming priest, weeks before he appears; including "testimonials" from parishioners in the church he's leaving. Thus they prepare his entry even as they say goodbye to their departing priest.

Leadership changes are often a time for innovation, and are sometimes met with resistance. The incoming pastor may have a vision of his own, and while most people are very polite they may not be especially enthusiastic. Appreciative Inquiry is a great tool for helping the pastor understand the parish's history and hopes, and for joining parish and pastor together to create a truly shared vision. Even with no prior preparation work, the new pastor can meet with the various leadership groups in the parish in an informal atmosphere and ask appreciative questions about past successes and about their wishes for the future of the parish.

NEWMAN CENTER, BUCKNELL UNIVERSITY

Many Catholic students attend secular universities, where Newman Centers connect them with other Catholics on campus. New school years create new leadership teams for these centers. At the Newman Center at Bucknell University in Lewisburg, PA, Fr. Marty Moran engaged Appreciative Inquiry consultant Therese Miller to help develop the student leadership for the Catholic Campus Ministry (CCM).

INTRODUCTORY QUESTIONS

The day of discernment was held outdoors on sets of four-person benches facing one another. After introductions in the whole group, students assembled on these benches, creating several eight-person groups. Each student interviewed the person next to them on the bench for five minutes, asking two basic appreciative questions:

• Best Experience: Tell me about the best times you have had with CCM. Looking at your entire experience, recall a time when you felt most alive, most involved, or most excited about your involvement. What made it an exciting experience? Who was involved? Describe the event in detail.

• What do you think is the core life-giving factor or value of CCM? What is it that, if it did not exist, would make CCM totally different than it currently is?

After these interviews each eight-person group shared high points of the stories they had heard and the ideas that "grabbed" them, then reported those themes to everyone else while Miller captured core values on a flip chart.

CREATING EXPERTS WITH ROTATIONAL INTERVIEWS

In circumstances where it is desirable for people to meet a large number of other participants, a rotating interview format can be used. Miller selected this method for further questions related to leadership. Each student was given four index cards, all with the same set of questions on only one of four topics (Wisdom, Vision, Power or Love). They were to become "experts" on that topic. By rotating their place on the bench, the students interviewed four peers (5 minutes each) using their particular topic questions. Miller explained, "As an interviewer you hear all the answers on one topic, but as an interviewee you are being interviewed on four different topics." The questions under the topics were:

• Wisdom: What strengths and values do you bring to your leadership role? How do you express these strengths and values in your life?

• Vision: What are your hopes for CCM? What are the aspirations you have for yourself as a leader of the CCM community?

• Power: What are your goals for this academic year? What are your personal goals? What will you do, and how will you be, to accomplish these goals?

• Love: What part of the CCM mission is most meaningful to you? What part of your work with CCM makes you feel most alive most fulfilled?

Group members jotted down notes from the interviews on individual note cards labeled with the interviewee's name.

EXPERTS GATHER FOR DATA ANALYSIS AND CREATE PROVOCATIVE PROPOSITIONS

Next, the topic 'experts' met for 30 minutes to share some of the stories they had heard, and to brainstorm a list of the key ideas or themes from the interviews. They were helped by the following questions specific to their topic:

Wisdom:
> • What is the wisdom of the CCM Steering Committee?
> • How does the CCM Steering Committee express its wisdom?

Vision:
> • What is the vision of the Steering Committee for CCM?
> • What is the vision that the CCM has for itself?

Power:
> • What does the CCM Steering Committee have the power to accomplish this year?
> • How will the CCM realize its power?

Love:
- What does the CCM Steering Committee love?
- How does the CCM Steering Committee express this love on campus and in the world?"

Miller bypassed the technical detail about how to write a provocative proposition by guiding students to write answers on flipcharts in this format:

- The wisdom (Vision/Power/Love) of the CCM steering committee is...
- The CCM Steering Committee expresses its wisdom (Vision/Power/Love) by...

The entire assembly then gathered to share the key ideas from all four topics. As the students looked at the data generated, they were able to see what was necessary for the CCM as a whole. After the group work was complete, everyone received their personal note cards. Reading over what they had said in the interviews, each took time alone to think about their words, to look for recurring personal themes, and to answer the following questions:

- What gift do I bring to the CCM Steering Committee?
- How do I offer this gift to the Committee, to CCM, and to the world?

They then wrote answers in this format:

- The gift that I bring is...
- I offer this gift by...

Students returned to the large group to share their discerned gifts with one another. Following this Appreciative Inquiry, Miller led the students in 3 hours of leadership training and planning using other methods. The planning that followed was built on the information gathered during the discovery, dream and discernment. Fr. Moran felt that the process affirmed the students as leaders but also helped them realize what they and the Newman Center needed to grow. He said, "They liked finding gifts they hadn't seen in themselves."

RESULTS

The day led to an unanticipated re-structuring of the way CCM is run. In the past, leadership was anyone who had a "warm body" that could be persuaded to fill the position. As a result of the retreat, the group emerged with a checklist of attributes for each position. Fr. Moran explained that now, it is acceptable to leave a position vacant until the right candidate emerges, and that they no longer "elect" leaders. "The new tactic is that we don't put someone in a position of leadership unless they've gone through a process of discernment themselves and then we've gone through it with them. It's a contract." Before the leadership seminar there were 23 members of the steering committee. Using the discernment processes, several dropped off, while others have been invited on, swelling the ranks to 32. Fr. Moran explained, "The workshop helped them gracefully step down and helped new leaders emerge. We didn't expect those who emerged to emerge." Appreciative Inquiry "helped empower the quieter leaders to step forward." In addition, the discernment helped leaders who are burning out to share the work, as they saw that they could concentrate on what they were good at, and let others do the same. "Now eight people are doing what two were doing before."

SACRED HEART-GRIFFIN HIGH SCHOOL:
Selecting a New Principal

Sacred Heart-Griffin (SHG) High School in Illinois used an appreciative process to develop criteria for choosing a new principal. Their selection method was a process of discovery into what type of person would most fit with their vision as a school. Under the leadership of President Marilyn Jean Runkel, O.P., the search committee asked one another questions such as:

• What do you value most about SHG as a school community?

• What do you consider to be the core life-giving factors of SHG?

• What is it you want most for SHG as we move into the future with a new model?

• What challenges do we need to be aware of as we proceed?

With the data gathered and analyzed by the group, the committee created provocative propositions about the future of SHG as they transitioned to a President-Principal model and searched for a principal. Here are two of the 10 criteria they developed:

1. "We seek strong Catholic and academic credentials with positive commitment toward faith, faculty and family."

2. "We desire a collaborative mode of leadership committed to a team approach. We see SHG as innovative, progressive, and proactive, on the cutting edge."

Based on their provocative propositions, they created a 15-item checklist with which to rate each candidate. In addition to basic experience and credential items, the checklist included strength in faith commitment, commitment to a team approach, and compassion and fairness. The items were marked on a scale from outstanding to unsatisfactory. This checklist resulted in a selection well matched to their most heartfelt needs.

TRANSITION INTO MARRIAGE

Pre-Cana programs to prepare people for the transition into marriage are widely used. Yet many engaged couples are turned off by an emphasis on all of the problems the couple will encounter. Pre-Cana programs built on Appreciative Inquiry would emphasize the couple's resilience and ability to cope with stress together. The couple might look at positive questions such as:

• What attracted you to one another? What is it about the other that caused you to say, she or he is the one?

• Tell me about a time when you were able to resolve a difficult difference of opinion, so that the outcome pleased you both.

• Without being humble, what are the strengths you believe that you personally bring to the marriage?

• What are the qualities you see in your partner that will strengthen the marriage?

• What, to you, is the essence of your relationship, the part of who you are that makes your relationship what it is?

• Imagine it is 30 years from now, and you have a stable and happy marriage, a model of cooperation, mutual respect and love. Describe the three things that made it possible.

As in other Appreciative Inquiry processes, a couple can pull the core themes out of the answers to these questions, thus clarifying important values prior to marriage. They can do dream work, picturing where they see themselves in five or ten years and develop a vision for their own future.

TRANSITION TIMES WITHIN MARRIAGE AND BEYOND

After all our grown children had left home, my husband and I participated in an appreciative couples retreat led by author Jane Watkins and her husband, Ralph Kelly. After answering questions similar to those above, we used art to develop our common vision. We worked separately to create visual images of an ideal future, shared those with one another, and then took tempera paints and silently worked together to create one shared image. From that we crafted a vision statement or provocative proposition for our marriage: "We are lifetime lovers who happily partner to create and preserve an open space where we can realize our individual and collective dreams." The Design Phase involves asking individuals to consider and commit what next step they are willing to do to bring about the preferred future.

Appreciative processes can be easily added to existing programs for couples and families, and to develop new programs for families at every stage, including single parents, the divorced and widowed. While I found no examples such as this yet being used in the Church, they are a natural outgrowth of a more positive approach. Bill Boomer, of the Department of Marriage and Family Ministry at the Diocese of Cleveland said his department is "growing into using Appreciative Inquiry in family ministry. I was traditionally trained to focus on problems. My wife taught me that people are not problems to be solved but persons to be loved. AI shows that all families have strengths." Boomer wants to "move away from myths that healthy families have no problems or that the only ideal family is 2 parents etc." and to emphasize family resiliency, "helping them see their strengths, generating a new way for them to see themselves as a connected group of people who have resources." He wants parishes to "see all families as holy." The overall effect of the appreciative approach on issues both large and small —whether moving from one pastor or principal or from one mode of life to another is a method that brings more life and hope to enhance transitions.

CHAPTER 6

GROWING FAITH

Using Appreciative Inquiry

for Spiritual Renewal

GROWING FAITH
Using Appreciative Inquiry for Spiritual Renewal

RESPECTFUL LISTENING

 One of the assumptions underlying Appreciative Inquiry is the Poetic Principle: the idea that there are multiple valid interpretations of what is read, seen, and heard. Interpreting a poem, Scripture, or the words and actions of a person, organization, community or nation occurs through the lens of our current development and worldview. In AI we learn to listen to ourselves and to one another in an open way, suspending judgment as we hear a variety of views. Because we are no longer defending ourselves, we can arrive at a deeper self-understanding. This kind of respectful listening is a prerequisite to reflective and generative dialogue.[1]

Positive participatory dialogue is more effective than either lecture or debate at enhancing personal awareness, spiritual growth and unity. As Pope Paul VI said, *"You can tell me that one can be satisfied with proclaiming the message ... but for a fully conscious humanity, adult and often adverse, preaching, which is a monologue, is not enough. The other must be heard, one must put oneself in his place."*[2] The loving atmosphere that grows out of appreciative dialogue makes a wonderful tool for spiritual retreats. Maria Elena Uribe says parish council spiritual retreats using Appreciative Inquiry are "the most exciting thing I've ever seen."

Uribe tells of one man who sat in the back of the room at the start of his "umpteenth required retreat." After finding himself drawn into the AI group he confessed, "I had planned to take a nap, but this was so interesting I couldn't even think of blinking!" The interest comes from discovering one's own deep spirituality and the harmonious values of others in the church through the uniquely structured process of sharing and dialogue. People who may have served the same church or council and never known the depth and beauty of the people they work with can get to know one another spiritually.

GROUP PRAYER SERVICES AND SPIRITUAL REFLECTION

The Diocese of Cleveland Self-Study Resources for Vibrant Parish Life suggests using appreciative questions for reflection in group prayer services. Their suggested questions can be asked of the group as a whole or be used in one-on-one interviews.

- How is God at work in our diocese right now?
- What is God asking of us in our place and time?
- How is God at work in my life right now, and what is God asking of me?
- How can I as an individual and we as a group more fully serve the reign of God?

In a one- or two-hour Bible study any passage can be discussed appreciatively, in small groups or as a whole. After reading and clarifying the language and context of the passage, Discovery questions might inquire about personal meanings and applications.

If the Bible Study is focusing, for example, on John (15:12) — *"This is my commandment, that you love one another as I have loved you,"* appropriate appreciative questions might include the following:

- Tell a story from your own experience that best illustrates the application of this commandment to love one another. As you reflect on that incident, what is the most important thing you learned from it?
- We develop our understanding of God's Word over time, gradually learning deeper meanings and applying it to our lives. Right now, what does the passage mean to you? What could lead you to an even deeper understanding?
- Imagine that in the future you have taken this passage to heart and learned to love others as Jesus has loved you. What difference would this make in your life? In the life of your loved ones?
- In the future, we will continue to learn about how to apply these words to our own faith community. If there were one small step you personally could take toward loving others within our parish, what would that small step be?

With additional time, such a Bible study can expand into a half-day retreat. After an opening prayer and Mass (if possible), begin the Discovery process:

DISCOVERY

- Read John (15:1-17) and related passages (places Scripture in context for fuller understanding).
- Briefly clarify language/context of the times. Suggest how to do contemplative prayer.
- Read John (15:12) again followed by silent contemplative prayer (15 minutes).
- Give attendees copies of the full passage and the interview questions outlined above. Ask attendees to read the questions and then privately contemplate their answers (45 minutes).
- Alternate: If a labyrinth is readily available, read the questions and contemplate them privately while walking the labyrinth.

- Break into groups of two and conduct interviews using the same questions (30 minutes per interview, one hour total).
- Join each group of two with another. Tell the high points of what was heard and note on flip charts key themes from the stories (30 minutes).
- Come together as a whole group and look at themes. Have the group extract core values and meanings of the passage in their lives. Give each person three sticky dots or stars and have them place those on the themes most important to them at this time (30 minutes).
- Make a new clean list of the core values.

DREAM

In this spiritual work, dreaming is not movement toward a goal for the organization, but rather a way to help people come out of the retreat with a greater sense of that passage. Some Dream exercises might include the following:
- Join with another group of four to make a group of eight. Invite members to imagine the themes articulated in Discovery being fully present in their lives and church community and, what that would look like. Use various provided art materials to create together a visual metaphor of that ideal state of being (30 minutes).
- Share images with the whole group. Energy in the group will be very high at this point.
- Facilitator can summarize both the creativity and commonalities in images. Congratulate groups. Ask the whole group to contemplate for two minutes how their understanding of the passage has grown as the day has progressed, and then share some of those insights.
- Have people express appreciation to one another for the gifts received.

BRINGING SPIRITUALITY INTO THE WORKPLACE[3]

A glance at the business section of any large bookstore reveals that work and spirituality is a hot topic[4]. Fueled by corporate scandals, unemployment, and the universal search for meaning in chaotic times, people want ways to keep their souls alive in their work. In 1986, The Reverend Norm Douglas, a priest of the Diocese of Cleveland, and attorney Larry Vuillemin discovered common ground in their search for a greater synergy between work and spirituality. One man was reflecting on how a person's work life could be linked more strongly with personal beliefs and values. The other was looking for ways to make the faith of individual believers more relevant and practical at work. Together, they explored ways to incorporate ethics into our everyday world, and to bridge the gap between spirituality and daily "busyness."

They started Heart to Heart Communications[5], a not-for-profit organization in Akron, Ohio, with the purpose of strengthening connections people have to "our deeper selves, to core ethical values, to the meaning and purpose of our work, and to one another." The organization, they say, is about "active spirituality — a spirituality that influences why and how we do our daily tasks. We connect the spiritual with the practical, bringing people together to enrich and support one another in living our ideals, especially at work."

In 2002-03 in greater Akron, Heart to Heart used Appreciative Inquiry to interview more than 80 leaders from a variety of professions, businesses, government, not-for-profit, and community organizations. The videotaped interviews generated powerful insights. The questions included the following:
• Tell us about a time when you felt most alive, most purposeful, most excited about your work. Who or what made it so? What were the most important factors about the organization that helped to make this a vital experience?
• How have ethics played a role in this experience?
• As a leader, what resources do you rely on to stay inspired in your work and your ongoing development?
• What are the personal/spiritual practices you have found most useful?

RESULTS

Taped interview highlights and a book of quotes from every interview were shared at the 10th annual breakfast attended by over 500 community leaders, Greater Akron Speaks out for Values, in April 2003. "Our purpose for conducting the interviews was to engage leaders in the Akron area in the conversation about what fosters vital, ethical, purposeful workplaces and work leadership," says Fr. Douglas. Both Vuillemin and Douglas feel that the dialogue is off to a positive and productive start.

CHAPTER 7

A WIDER VIEW

Appreciative Inquiry

in Other Faith

Communities

A WIDER VIEW
Appreciative Inquiry in Other Faith Communities

FOSTERING INTERFAITH RELATIONSHIPS

Days after 9/11/01 The Rev. Paul Chaffee, a United Church of Christ minister, facilitated a public discussion including a Christian seminary president, a rabbi, and two Muslim community leaders. He began by asking each participant, "What is it that makes your faith so precious to you?" Then he asked "about the gifts, the wisdom, and insights each of your extraordinary traditions has to offer us about peace, about comforting the afflicted, about justice, about living when there is no justice, and about relating to the stranger." Because his questions searched out the positives, the 150 participants representing a dozen different faiths were able to discuss tough issues respectfully.

For Chaffee, Appreciative Inquiry turned out to be a perfect methodology for growing a faith community, for fostering cooperation between faith communities, and for living out Gospel values, even in crisis. The evening resulted in a plan to come together across faith divisions on a regular basis "to learn from each other, and to give their local community a new kind of religious voice." He finds that in his interfaith work he needn't specifically explain the methodology, but that just doing the work relaxes people's fears and prejudices about one another.

The Rev. Chaffee is also the founding director of the Interfaith Center in the Presidio in San Francisco, where he teaches Appreciative Inquiry to faith and interfaith communities. Many Biblical passages suggest welcoming outsiders into friendship, such as Deuteronomy (10:19) *"You shall also love the stranger, for you were strangers in the land of Egypt"* and Matthew (25:35) where Jesus says *"I was a stranger and you welcomed me..."* Reflecting such passages, Rev. Chaffee says that AI helps us "recognize the assets of strangers" and could lead to a world "less dominated by division."

CLERGY LEADERSHIP INSTITUTE: *Leadership Training*

The Rev. Rob Voyle developed the Clergy Leadership Institute (CLI)[1] to aid Episcopal and other clergy in transitioning from the model of a pastor as counselor or spiritual director for individuals, to a model of pastors as leaders of dynamic congregations. CLI offers a yearlong leadership training program to clergy in active ministry, as well as shorter programs in Appreciative Inquiry. The Rev. Voyle says he has found little resistance to AI among clergy because Christian theology is consistent with developing "an appreciative way of being in the world." The AI focus on values and discovering how to live out our core values is a deeply spiritual activity. The Rev. Voyle believes that because AI is mission-focused, increasing the use of it in the Church could take the Body of Christ "from maintenance to mission."

AI IN THE EPISCOPAL CHURCH

Many Episcopal clergy have experienced the power of Appreciative Inquiry firsthand through work with consultant Helen Spector. Diocese of Newark Bishop Right Reverend John P. Croneberger called Spector to help restructure his staff. She asked the bishop about the work of the unit he wanted to restructure. He answered, "The work of the staff is to support the work of the people of the diocese." As a Jew, Spector feels the freedom to ask questions that people within the faith might consider too elementary. "And what is the work of the people of the diocese?" she asked. Following a lengthy pause, Spector reports that the bishop answered, "That's really the question, isn't it?"

Spector's insightful question led to an Appreciative Inquiry into "the work of the people of the diocese." "I do believe," she says, "that the way we frame the first questions and the search for the core values in an AI actually shifts the boundary, in most cases, away from those which keep our attention focused on what doesn't work, and causes us to include people in the inquiry who we never would have considered part of the system under the old ways of looking at things."

Expanding our boundaries and ideas about who is involved as part of a system increases the possibilities of growth and positive change. Spector says that one of the most common remarks from the interviews was that "through the stories people had come to know others they never thought they'd want to be in conversation with. Just by pairing them with people they don't know, all of a sudden — because of our common humanity and what our faith life means to us— the larger whole can contain us."

Appreciative Inquiry's fundamental methodology of beginning with a story and moving on to a vision is basic to Christianity and other Scripture-based religions. "The people of the Book are people of story," Spector says. At the end of the Visioning Convocation Spector led, the Newark Diocesan management team asked her, "Where do we go from here?" In one of his columns[2] Bishop Croneberger reported that her answer was "Give in to your hopes, not your fears." The Bishop went on to compare that appreciative quote with the drama of Holy Week, and the hope-filled, life-giving proclamation of the resurrection.

EXECUTIVE COUNCIL: *Transition Management*

Appreciative Inquiry consultant and author Bernard J. Mohr[3] has worked with the Executive Council of the Episcopal Church, USA, in transition management. Because one-half of the council leaders turn over every three years, the new council spends three days "walking through the process of clarifying roles, establishing a vision for how they want to work together, and modifying their internal organization to reflect changing priorities, etc." Mohr uses an AI Discovery protocol to facilitate the council meetings. Here is a condensed version:

1. As you think back over your history with the church, tell me a story about one of those special moments when you felt that you were really alive and contributing to others around you—a time when you felt particularly excited about your involvement in the church, when you were affirmed in your commitment to being part of this institution. What made it a peak experience?

2. Common sense suggests that when people are able to mesh their talents, gifts and passions with the work that needs to be done, both the work of this council and we as individuals are enriched. Without being humble, tell me what you value deeply about yourself as an individual and perhaps also as a member of the church.

3. Without being humble, tell me what you believe are the special gifts that you would like to offer this community, and this executive council as it moves forward to address the many challenges it will face.

4. The last question focused on you as an individual. I'd now like to focus on the executive council as a living entity —an entity that has a history of enabling traditions as well as a potential future capability that is yet to be developed. Please tell me which of the council's traditions have been most life-giving and tell me a story of one time when that tradition was enacted.

5. As we face into a new triennium, with new council members and new leadership, the opportunity for creating new relationships, new levels of collaboration between council and staff, is very high. What hopes do you have for how council and staff work together? Give me a past example of what it actually looked like when council and staff were working together in the most collaborative and effective way possible.

6. The executive council, like every human organization, has some one element, some one thing without which its spirit would wither. What, in your opinion, is that core factor that gives vitality and life to the executive council — the one thing that is important for us to retain, to bring with us as we move into the future?

7. One of our goals this week is to establish preferred operating norms. What two to three agreements about how we work together, would support and enhance the core life-giving force that you identified in the last question?

8. Creating the future we prefer involves not only highlighting the best of our past and expanding those capabilities into a vision of the future, but creating a council that is alive and effective and that uses the talents and gifts of all of those here. If you had a magic wand with three wishes that could help you to be the council member or staff member that you would most like to be, what three things would you wish for?

RESULTS

The three days of discovery, dreaming and designing quickly create the foundation for an effective team. As an early adopter of Appreciative Inquiry, the Episcopal Church offers a history rich with experiences to study. Many other faith communities — both Christian and non-Christian — are now experimenting with this positive approach.

CHAPTER 8

INVITATION

Appreciative Inquiry

as a Paradigm Shift

INVITATION TO USE APPRECIATIVE INQUIRY
Appreciative Inquiry as a Paradigm Shift

Changing our view of the world is a process. Four hundred years ago Descartes and Newton conceived of the world as a machine with separate parts. Through this view, we pay more attention to division than wholeness, and to the issues between us than to the ways we connect. That worldview is a paradigm, a lens through which our secular Western civilization has viewed everything. Although that view is contradicted by both modern science and Scripture, we are all conditioned to the idea, as Deborah Tannen says in *The Argument Culture*, that "the best way to show you're really smart is to criticize."[1]

Appreciative Inquiry looks at ways to find connections and wholeness. Today we know that every "part" is connected with every other part, and that we are connected with one another. Jesus preceded holistic thinking with his bold assertion about the Body of Christ: *"I am the vine and you are the branches. Those who abide in me and I in them bear much fruit, because apart from me you can do nothing"* (John 15:5).

Since connection is a fact, we might more closely follow St. Paul's advice in Romans (14:13-19): *"Let us therefore no longer pass judgment on one another, but resolve instead never to put a stumbling block or hindrance in the way of another ... Let us then pursue what makes for peace and for mutual upbuilding."*

Pope Paul VI, commenting on his encyclical Ecclesium Suam, saw loving dialogue as a means by which the church could remain united. Just as families must discuss things openly to remain true to one another, that same need exists both within the Body of Christ and between the church and the world. In *The Pope Speaks*[2], he said;

"It is that common love of truth which is the only reason for the existence of the sincere dialogue of which I am speaking, and which has little in common with worldly dialogues, which only seek a display of one's wit, and if one is able, that of others ... If there is always inequality of situation, there is always equality of intention; an act of pure love, for example, makes the sinner and the just instantly equal. In the same way the absolute love of truth immediately makes equal those who seek together."

"The world outside the church decks itself in the most seductive colors. And the Catholic world seems small, mean, and colorless. One sees all the

deficiencies. And then, instead of making common cause with ones own people, it is on the contrary with strangers to Catholicism that one allies oneself, to criticize what goes on at home. And by a strange though tempting reversal, one is closer to those outside than those within, one fraternizes with strangers, while cutting oneself off from one's brethren."

"That is a pity. That is not the Church's way. For to give the church to the world, the church must first of all be a living church; that is, a united, fraternal community where each is joined to the others—those with pastoral duties, those who make up the faithful. I do not wish to utter the words discipline, obedience. I know they are not liked in our time because of their former connotation. But ... what the word obedience, or better, the word fidelity designates is something no living community can dispense with. I mean an obedience full of respect, an active, joyous, intelligent, open fidelity, a fidelity which can be a state of dialogue."

Mary Pat Frey of Painesville, Ohio, finds that even after a lot of exposure to Appreciative Inquiry there can still be a tendency in some people to drift back into the old problem-solving mode and to "focus on the strengths-and-weaknesses analysis instead of thinking about gifts and wishes." She is not dissuaded. "The future using AI will be wonderful," she says. "But the challenge will be really getting people to embrace it, commit to it, pass it down, teach it, and have it become part of how we do all things."

Rick Krivanka emphasizes that Appreciative Inquiry is not just a new paradigm but a very different one. "Some people may think that asking a few questions that are perceived as positive and soft is the distinguishing factor that makes a process Appreciative Inquiry. But AI is in fact a completely different model." To illustrate, Krivanka tells the story of a pastor who called him because he was concerned with the negativity of the comments at a recent parish "town-hall" meeting. Krivanka learned that the question the pastor had asked parishioners was "What are your concerns?" Indeed, they told him! Naturally their concerns were all problem-oriented. Paradigm-shifting questions would be: *What most gives life to our parish? What would you like to see happen to bring forth the best of life and vitality in our future?*

Changing the way we question is important if we are to adopt a positive worldview; so is getting people to accept that a "nice" approach can be effective. David DeLambo believes that the hardest thing in convincing a parish to try Appreciative Inquiry is to get them over the idea that AI is a way of glossing over conflict. "What we constantly say is that normal problem solving focuses on what people do not want, not on what they do want," DeLambo says. "At the heart of any conflict is something that people value or cherish — the thing they are not getting. When AI asks questions that allow people to share a best moment or a high point when they most fully experienced the reality they desire, [people can] speak directly and concretely to what matters most. AI does not mask conflict, it reframes it constructively."

"Some people thought Appreciative Inquiry was like Pollyanna," says Terry Ryan, a parishioner at St. Justin Martyr in Eastlake, Ohio, "but it was a really good process." In her experience, people cynical about AI "think we should focus on problems because we have so many of them to deal with." Ryan understands this approach to traditional strategic planning from her work in government and business, but believes if you deal with what's good and healthy and gives life to the parish, solutions to the problem will appear during the process. "As we went along in the process we had a number of people who had received the pastor's letter about it and they would call the parish, and ask, 'Can I be interviewed?'" Her parish is still working with the data from the interviews and people are eager to go further. "There is curiosity," Ryan says, "and that is a positive impact."

Far from being Pollyanna, Appreciative Inquiry does get at the problems — but from another direction. Krivanka firmly believes that AI is "not a dodge. We're not evading anything. What we are helping people do is to shine light on what they deeply cherish and care about. This approach gets you to the deeper issues."

When the old paradigm falls away, we can focus on the present and future instead of the problems of the past. Appreciative Inquiry accomplishes that by affirming connections and prompting growth in our organizations, our communities, and ourselves. This need not always be done on a large scale to be effective. We can change our worldview one individual at a time. Although in this book we've looked at examples of well-crafted projects involving many people, the philosophy can become your own through the small steps you take to live it in your daily life. We can begin this "discipline of appreciation" today simply by looking for the good, the true, and the beautiful around us. You can begin to use Appreciative Inquiry by asking just one appreciative question at the beginning of your next parish meeting such as: Since our last meeting, where have you noticed God at work in our ministry[3]? Or at the end of any meeting ask, what did we as a group do well today? Small steps like this begin to highlight the life-giving properties of the Church. As Pope John XXIII who convened Vatican II said:

"Consult not your fears, but your hopes and dreams.

Think not about your frustrations,

but about your unfulfilled potential.

Concern yourself not with what you tried and

failed in, but with what it is still possible for you to do."

— Pope John XXIII

Endnotes

CHAPTER 1: APPRECIATIVE INQUIRY
A Path to Positive Change

[1] Except where part of a quote from an encyclical or other source, all Scripture quotations contained herein are from the *New Revised Standard Version Bible*, copyright 1989 by the Division of Christian Education of the National Council of the Churches of Christ in the USA and are used with permission. All rights reserved. The author used *The New Oxford Annotated Bible*, 3rd edition, *New Revised Standard Version with the Apocrypha*, Oxford U. Press, 2001.

[2] Case has a marvelous website, full of content practitioners have shared. See resources for the address.

[3] Reprinted with permission from *The Thin Book of ®Appreciative Inquiry.*

[4] Jossey-Bass/Pfeiffer, 2001.

[5] See *Lessons from the Field: Applying Appreciative Inquiry* from www.thinbook.com.

[6] Although there is a book out with a compilation of questions used for many topics. See Resources for Diana Whitney et al, *Encyclopedia of Positive Questions.*

CHAPTER 2: COMPATIBILITY
The Link Between Appreciative Inquiry and the Catholic Church

[1] Peter Henriot et al, *Catholic Social Teaching: Our Best Kept Secret*, Orbis Books, 1988

[2] All quotes from US Conference of Catholic Bishops, Excerpts from Sharing Catholic Social Teaching (USCCB website, http://www.nccbuscc.org/)

[3] See *Lessons from the Field: Applying Appreciative Inquiry,* Thin Book Publishing, 1998, 2001, p. 12.

[4] http://papal-library.saintmike.org/PaulVI/Encyclicals/Ecclesiam_Suam.html

[5] a Catholic priest of the Congregation of the Mission (Vincentians) in the Philippines and Vice President for Administration of Adamson University.

[6] Thin Book Publishing, 1998, 2001

[7] Rick and David have written about Appreciative Inquiry in *Four Ways to Build More Effective Parish Councils* edited by Mark Fischer and Margaret Raley (Twenty-third Publications, 2002).

[8] Austin Flannery, Editor, "Lumen Gentium" in Vatican Council II, Volume I The Conciliar and Post Conciliar Documents, (Costello, Dominican, 1975, 1998) Vatican II, 11/21/1964, n.32, 33

CHAPTER 3: REACHING OUT
Using Appreciative Inquiry to Build Relationships and Community

[1] Available from PACT Publications (www.pactpublications.com).

[2] GEM stands for Global Excellence in Management and is a project of Case Western Reserve University's Weatherhead School of Management. It has been an outstanding pioneer of Appreciative Inquiry since its inception. For more information visit ai.cwru.edu/practice/non-profit.cfm.

[3] These follow the "classic" Appreciative Inquiry questions. You will see versions of these questions throughout the book.

[4] Ultimately Appreciative Inquiry like any change process asks people to change their behavior. See Jack Britain's "Do we really mean it?" in *Lessons from the Field* on the dynamics of behavior change.

[5] *Lessons from the Field* includes a chapter on Imagine Chicago by Bliss Browne.

[6] Thanks to Rick Krivanka for his input into this section.

CHAPTER 4 PLANNING
Using AI for Strategic Planning and Creating Mission Statements

[1] (www.chac.ca) In 2003, CHAC membership included seven provincial associations; 31 sponsors/owners of health care organizations; 112 hospitals and homes; health care professionals; and affiliate organizations and individuals.

[2] Reprinted from *The Catholic Health Ministry: Living Icons of Compassion. The National Dialogue Findings* available at www.chac.ca.

[3] Ms. Keon is Vice-Chair of CHAC, Chair of National Dialogue Steering Committee and Vice President of Clinical Programs at Pembroke General Hospital in Pembroke, Ontario.

[4] RHSJ Health Centre of Cornwall, Ontario.

[5] Theology Professor Mark F. Fischer, PhD is Director of Admissions at St. John's Seminary in Camarillo, CA, and an expert on Parish Council Planning (see Resources). The *Today's Parish* article is available at www.west.net/~fischer.

[6] The few negative evaluations seemed to relate to some variability of the table facilitators, which underscores how important it is in any Appreciative Inquiry process that the facilitators be fully trained and have experienced the process themselves For AI training information contact the author or visit www.catholicappreciativeinquiry.com or www.thinbook.com.

[7] Henri Lacordaire from *On the Establishment in France of the Order of Preachers*.

[8] For an introduction to chaos theory, see Meg Wheatley's book, *Leadership and the New Science: Discovering Order in a Chaotic World*.

[9] Thanks to Michelle Smith of Brulant and again thanks to Rick Krivanka for this example.

[10] Coesfeld is the town in Germany where this community of the Sisters of Notre Dame were founded.

CHAPTER 6: GROWING FAITH
Using Aprreciative Inquiry for Spiritual Renewal

[1] See William Isaacs, *Dialogue and the Art of Thinking Together* (Currency/Doubleday, 1998) Isaacs sees suspension of judgment as the first critical choice point that turns conversation away from debate to generative dialogue. The second choice point is to choose reflection rather than objective analysis of what is heard.

[2] From Jean Guitton, *The Pope Speaks: Dialogues of Paul VI* (Meredith Press, 1968) p 174.

[3] Once again we thank Rick Krivanka for this example.

[4] I invite you to see my book on spirituality in the workplace, *Mystic in the Marketplace: Turning Work into Worship* (www.1stBooks.com) that compares the spiritual development of Catholic saints with the spiritual development of organizations. Work related, spiritually based questions conclude each chapter and can be used as the basis for individual or group study on this topic.

[5] http://www.h2hc.org.

CHAPTER 7: A WIDER VIEW
Appreciative Inquiry In Other Faith Communities

[1] See their website at www.clergyleadership.com.

[2] From *The Voice*, Diocese of Newark, April, 2001. Available at www.dioceseofnewark.org/jpc-0401.html.

[3] See Watkins and Mohr, *Appreciative Inquiry*, Jossey-Bass, 2001.

CHAPTER 8: INVITATION TO USE APPRECIATIVE INQUIRY
Appreciative Inquiry as a Paradigm Shift

[1] Deborah Tannen, *The Argument Culture: Stopping America's War of Words* (Ballentine Books, 1999, p8.

[2] From Jean Guitton, *The Pope Speaks: Dialogues of Paul VI* (Meredith Press, 1968) p167-178.

[3] Thanks to Gail Roussey for this question.

RESOURCES

Bibliography

Catholic Health Association of Canada, *The Catholic Health Ministry: Living Icons of Compassion.* The National Dialogue Findings available at www.chac.ca.

Catholic Relief Services, *The Partnership Toolbox: A Facilitator's Guide to Partnership* Dialogue PACT Publications (www.pactpublications.com)

Croneberger, Bishop John, "Give Into Your Hopes, Not your Fears" April, 2001 column "The Bishop's Message" in *The Voice,* available at www.dioceseofnewark.org.

Flannery, Austin, Editor, "Lumen Gentium" in Vatican Council II, Volume I The Conciliar and Post Conciliar Documents, (Costello, Dominican, 1975, 1998)

Fischer, Mark F., PhD, *Today's Parish* article January 1997 is available at his Parish Pastoral Councils website under the title, "Appreciative Leadership". www.west.net/~fischer.

The New Oxford Annotated Bible: New Revised Standard Version, 3rd edition (Oxford University Press, 2001)

Guitton, Jean, *The Pope Speaks: Dialogues of Paul VI* (Meredith Press, 1968)

Hammond, Sue Annis, *The Thin Book of® Appreciative Inquiry,* (Thin Book Publishing, 1996, 1998) from www.thinbook.com

Hammond, Sue Annis and Cathy Royal, PhD, Editors, *Lessons from the Field: Applying Appreciative Inquiry,* (Thin Book Publishing, 1998, 2000) from www.thinbook.com

Henriot, Peter et al, *Catholic Social Teaching: Our Best Kept Secret,* Orbis Books, 1988

Isaacs, William, *Dialogue and the Art of Thinking Together* (Currency/Doubleday, 1998)

Krivanka, Rick and David DeLambo, " Appreciative Inquiry" in *Four Ways to Build More Effective Parish Councils* edited by Mark Fischer and Margaret Raley (Twenty-third Publications, 2002).

Bibliography

Lacordaire, Henri , *On the Re-Establishment in France of the Order of Preachers.* Quoted at Springfield Dominicans website, www.springfieldop.org

Paddock, Susan Star, *Mystic in the Marketplace: Turning Work into Worship* (www.1stBooks.com, 2002)

Pope Paul VI, *Ecclesium Suam*, reprinted at http://papal-library.saint-mike.org/PaulVI/Encyclicals/Ecclesiam_Suam.html

Tannen, Deborah, *The Argument Culture: Stopping America's War of Words* (Ballentine Books, 1999)

US Conference of Catholic Bishops, Excerpts from *Sharing Catholic Social Teaching* (USCCB website, http://www.nccbuscc.org/)

Watkins, Jane and Bernard J.Mohr *Appreciative Inquiry: Change at the Speed of Imagination* (Jossey-Bass/Pfeiffer, 2001)

Wheatley, Meg, *Leadership and the New Science: Discovering Order in a Chaotic World* (Berrett-Koehler, 1992)

Whitney, Diana, David Cooperrider, Amanda Trosten-Bloom, Brian S. Kaplin *Encyclopedia of Positive Questions: Using AI to Bring out the Best in Your Organization* (Lakeshore Communications, 2002)

For Further Study

- *The Thin Book of® Appreciative Inquiry*, Sue Annis Hammond. Small enough to serve as an easy introduction. (Thin Books) http://www.thinbook.com
- *Appreciative Inquiry: Change at the Speed of Imagination*, Jane Magruder Watkins, Bernard Mohr (Jossey-Bass, 2001) Very clear explanation of 5 steps with examples.
- T*he Power of Appreciative Inquiry: A Practical Guide to Positive Change*, Diana Whitney and Amanda Trosten-Bloom (Berrett Koehler 2003) Great introduction and explanation.
- *Locating the Energy for Change: An Introduction to Appreciative Inquiry*, Charles Elliott (IISD, 1999) in depth book with cases.
- *Lessons from the Field: Applying Appreciative Inquiry*, Sue Hammond and Cathy Royal, editors. (Thin Books 2001) Lots of great cases!
- *Encyclopedia of Positive Questions: Using AI to Bring out the Best in Your Organization*, David Cooperrider, Diana Whitney, Amanda Trosten-Bloom, Brian Kaplin. (Lakeshore Communications, 2001)
- *The Partnership Toolbox: A Facilitator's Guide to Partnership Dialogue*, Catholic Relief Services, (PACT Publications, www.pactpublications.com)
- *Four Ways to Build More Effective Parish Councils: A Pastoral Approach*, edited by Mark Fischer and Mary Raley, (Twenty-Third Publications, 2002) Contains chapter by Rick Krivanka and David DeLambo.
- *Appreciative Inquiry*, David Cooperrider and Diana Whitney (Berrett-Koehler, 1999) Another brief introduction.
- *The Appreciative Inquiry Handbook*, David Cooperrider, Diana Whitney, Jacqueline Stavros (Lakeshore Communications, 2003) Huge collection of examples, agendas, protocols and participant material. Comes with a CD of overheads. Available at www.thinbook.com

Helpful Websites
(Check for updates on www.catholicappreciativeinquiry.com)

- http://appreciativeinquiry.cwru.edu/ Start here. The Case Western Reserve University Website with multiple links. This site offers a huge bibliography and many downloadable helps.
- http://www.dioceseofcleveland.org/vibrantparishlife/, Tells about a dynamic community- based AI project to revitalize Catholic parish life.
- http://www.west.net/~fischer/A35.htm, parish pastoral councils website and 1997 article on appreciative inquiry by Mark Fischer.
- www.chac.ca, The story of a nationwide Appreciative Inquiry dialogue on health from the Catholic Health Association of Canada.
- www.catholicappreciativeinquiry.com, Use of AI within the Catholic Church. Please check here for an updated list of consultants and resources.
- www.nbccongress.org/black-catholic-monthiy/06-2003/appreciative-inquiry-01. asp. National Black Catholic Congress AI Project.

- www.imaginechicago.org, Imagine Chicago is an attempt to apply AI to the problems of a large city. Its successes have spurred Imagine Dallas, Imagine Africa, Imagine Garfield Heights, etc.
- www.h2hc.org, Heart to Heart Communications, Akron based spirituality, work dialogue.
- www.clergyleadership.com, Excellent resource for clergy who want to learn AI http://lists.business.utah.edu/mailman/listinfo/ailist, There is a listserve that you can join where questions are discussed, projects shared and events announced.
- www.thinbook.com, Good resource for books and information.

Brief Alphabetical List of Appreciative Inquiry Consultants Mentioned in this Book. (For Up-To-Date EMails or Contact Information Visit www.catholicappreciativeinquiry.com or EMail info@thinbook.com)

- Fr. Gregg Banaga Jr., C.M. Manila, Philippines, glbanaga@hotmail.com
- Paul Chaffee, San Francisco, CA, PJCHAFFEE@aol.com
- Sr. Margaret Crowley, RSM, West Hartford, CT, mcrowley@snet.net
- Bro. Lawrence Fidelus, PhD., O Carm., Joliet, Il.,LFidelus@carmelnet.org
- Sue Annis Hammond, Plano, TX suehammond@thinbook.com
- Meg Kinghorn, Washington DC mkinghorn@pacthq.org
- Rick Krivanka, Gail Roussey, David De Lambo, Diocese of Cleveland Pastoral Planning Office, rkrivanka@dioceseofcleveland.org, www.diocese ofcleveland.org
- Claudia Liebler, Takoma Park, MD, cliebler@ntelos.net
- James D. Ludema, Ph.D, Geneva, IL, jludema@compuserve.com
- Therese M. Miller, Lewisburg, PA, tmm@horizonworkplace.com, www.horizonworkplace.com
- Bernard Mohr, Portland, Maine, bjmsynapse@aol.com
- Jennifer Nazaire, Washington, DC, jnazaire@catholicrelief.org
- Susan Star Paddock, Gettysburg, PA , susanpaddock@peoplepc.com
- Tana Paddock, Montreal, Quebec, Canada, sprung.rhythm@sympatico.ca
- Jacqueline Pelletier, Ottawa, ON, Canada, jacquelinepelletier@sympatico.ca
- Sr. Marilyn Jean Runkel, O.P., Springfield, IL, smjrunkel@shg.org, runkelmjop@earthlink.net
- Helen Spector, Oakland CA, helen6451@aol.com
- Maria Elena Uribe, Los Angeles, CA MEuribe1078@aol.com
- Rob Voyle, California, www.clergyleadership.com, rob@voyle.com
- Jane Watkins and Ralph Kelly, Williamsburg, VA, www.appreciativeinquiryunlimited.com, janewatkins@compuserve.com, ralphfkelly@cox.net
- For info on the Brulant program used by the Sisters of Notre Dame contact Michelle Smith, Cleveland, OH, Brulant, www.brulant.com, smith@brulant.com

- Inquire about times when things were at their best, or when an individual had a peak experience. For example: Tell me a story about a time when you felt most alive and proud of being a Catholic? 6
- Share a peak experience related to the topic one at a time. Examples from the topic areas include "Describe a time when you had an extraordinarily deep sense of community." "Describe a time when your ministry was most energizing and enlivening." "Name and describe a practice, idea, or symbol that most clearly images or defines 'us' in your mind and heart." 40
- Think of a time (a "peak experience") when you really felt most alive, most excited and most committed as a member of your local Vincentian community. What and when was that experience or incident? Why was it a "peak experience" for you? What role did you play in it? Who was with you? 41
- Best Experience: Tell me about the best times you have had with Catholic Campus Ministry. Looking at your entire experience, recall a time when you felt most alive, most involved, or most excited about your involvement. What made it an exciting experience? Who was involved? Describe the event in detail. 47
- As you think back over your history with the church, tell me a story about one of those special moments when you felt that you were really alive and contributing to others around you—a time when you felt particularly excited about your involvement in the church, when you were affirmed in your commitment to being part of this institution. What made it a peak experience? 62
- Stories of Faith and Life: Describe an experience at St. Christopher Parish when you felt most alive, most fulfilled, or most enthused about your parish. Share the story of this 'best moment.' What made it the best moment? Who were the significant others involved and why were they significant? 36

Inner-directed or Core Values

- Inquire about the strengths an individual brings to the situation or about core factors or values that determine the essence of who we are. For example: God gifts each of us with certain abilities. Without being humble, what strengths have you been given that enable you to contribute positively to our parish? 6
- What is the single most important thing our parish has contributed to your life? 6
- What do you value most about yourself as a Catholic? 6
- What do you value most about: Yourself; Your membership in the Congregation; Your present ministry/work/assignment? 41
- Take a bird's eye view of your local community. What do you think are your unique strengths as a community? What gives life to your community? 41

• What do you think is the core life-giving factor or value of Catholic Campus Ministry? What is it that, if it did not exist, would make Catholic Campus Ministry totally different than it currently is? 47

• Common sense suggests that when people are able to mesh their talents, gifts and passions with the work that needs to be done, both the work of this council and we as individuals are enriched. Without being humble, tell me what you value deeply about yourself as an individual and perhaps also as a member of the church. 62

• Without being humble, tell me what you believe are the special gifts that you would like to offer this community, and this executive council as it moves forward to address the many challenges it will face. 62

• The executive council, like every human organization, has some one element, some one thing without which its spirit would wither. What, in your opinion, is that core factor that gives vitality and life to the executive council — the one thing that is important for us to retain, to bring with us as we move into the future? 62

• Our Core Values: Based on these shared Stories of Faith and Life, what values best express who we are and what we stand for as a parish community? 36

Future-oriented or Three wishes:

• Inquire about wishes for what you'd like to see more of in the future. For example: If you could imagine or transform our parish in any way you wished, what one to three things would you like to see happen to enhance its life and vitality? 6

• Imagine your community five years from today. You have just been voted by the entire Congregation to be the "best" local community in the world. How did you deserve this title? What is your vision for your community? What is happening in your community that best expresses your deepest aspirations and dreams? State three wishes you have for your community that would build on your existing strengths. 41

• Creating the future we prefer involves not only highlighting the best of our past and expanding those capabilities into a vision of the future, but creating a council that is alive and effective and that uses the talents and gifts of all of those here. If you had a magic wand with three wishes that could help you to be the council member or staff member that you would most like to be, what three things would you wish for? 63

OTHER TOPICS (ALPHABETICAL BY TOPIC)

Acting on Our Strengths (CHAC)

Engaging and envisioning provides an opportunity to go beyond what we thought was possible. It is time to push the creative edges of possibility and to wonder about the ministry's greatest potential. 32

- You have identified some unique strengths that characterize the ministry. How do you think we could best act on these strengths as individuals, organizations and parish communities? 32
- What are your 3 wishes that would make the Catholic health ministry even more exceptional and unique? 32

Attentiveness to the Whole Person (CHAC)

We all have physical, social and spiritual needs that require attention. Healing takes into account the wholeness of the person, recognizing the interrelationship of body, mind, and spirit. Such an understanding of healing affirms the dignity of persons and recognizes that healing is more than simply curing disease. It can mean restoring confidence and pride, providing a sense of community, or helping someone to forgive. Those of us engaged in the Catholic health ministry strive to nurture health and healing by providing compassionate and holistic care. 31

- Tell me a story or share an experience when you gave or witnessed such attentiveness. 31
- What enabled that experience to happen? What was it about you, the other people with you, the organization, the situation, etc. that contributed? 31

Change of Pastor

- What are the qualities you value most in our outgoing pastor? In what ways has he helped you to embody those qualities in your own life? 46
- What do you value the most about our parish? 46
- What do you most want our new pastor to know about our parish? 46
- What are the three concrete wishes you have for our parish's future? 46
- When you have felt most welcomed before, what happened? 47

Collaboration/Operating Norms

- As we face into a new triennium, with new council members and new leadership, the opportunity for creating new relationships, new levels of collaboration between council and staff, is very high. What hopes do you have for how council and staff work together? Give me a past example of what it actually looked like when council and staff were working together in the most collaborative and effective way possible. 62
- One of our goals this week is to establish preferred operating norms. What two to three agreements about how we work together, would support and enhance the core life-giving force that you identified in the last question? 63

Community hiring a new principal

- What do you value most about Sacred Heart Griffin as a school community? 50
- What do you consider to be the core life-giving factors of Sacred Heart Griffin? 50
- What is it you want most for Sacred Heart Griffin as we move into the future with a new model? 50
- What challenges do we need to be aware of as we proceed? 50

Community/Imagine Garfield Heights

- How long have you lived in Garfield Heights? In this community? What first brought your family here? What's it like for you to live in this community? 22
- When you think about the whole city of Garfield Heights, are there particular places or people or images that represent the city to you? 22
- Thinking back over your Garfield Heights memories, what have been real high points for you as a citizen of this city — times when you felt most alive, proud, excited about being a part of this community? 22
- Why did these experiences mean so much to you? 22
- How would you describe the quality of life in Garfield Heights today? 22
- What changes in the city would you most like to see? What do you imagine your own role might be in helping to make this happen? Who could work with you? 22
- Close your eyes and imagine Garfield Heights, as you most want it to be a generation from now. What is it like? What do you see and hear? What are you proudest of having accomplished? 22
- As you think back over this conversation, what images stand out for you as capturing your hopes for this city's future? 22
- What do you think would be an effective process for getting people across the city talking and working together on behalf of Garfield Heights' future? Whom would you want to draw into a Garfield Heights conversation? 22

Continuing the Healing Ministry (CHAC)

Each day we see people who demonstrate dedication, perseverance and devotion in the compassionate care they provide. Such persons radiate commitment and enthusiasm. The Catholic health and healing ministry, rooted in gospel values, is at its best when it strives to free people from physical and spiritual suffering, enabling them to live more fully. 31

- Share a significant experience you have had in the healing ministry, or that you are aware of, that enabled someone to live more fully. 31
- What made this experience possible? What was it about you, the other people, the organization, the situation, etc. that contributed? 31

Daring to Meet Unmet Needs (CHAC)

Throughout the history of our country, women and men of deep faith have responded to unmet health and social needs. These pioneers shaped the future of the Catholic health ministry and of health and social services in Canada. We remember their daring, creativity and determination. Moved by the needs of their day, they planned wisely, trusted in God, and acted with confidence and hope. 31
- Tell me a story about someone who inspired you by their daring, trust or creativity in the healing ministry. 31
- Share about a time when you, or your organization, lived this same spirit. 31
- What made that experience possible? What was it about you, the people with you, the organization, the situation, etc. that contributed? 31

Interfaith

- What is it that makes your faith so precious to you? 60
- What are the gifts, the wisdom, and insights each of your extraordinary traditions has to offer us about peace, about comforting the afflicted, about justice, about living when there is no justice, and about relating to the stranger." 60

Love

- What part of the Catholic Campus Ministry mission is most meaningful to you? What part of your work with Catholic Campus Ministry makes you feel most alive, most fulfilled? 48

Marriage

- What attracted you to one another? What is it about the other that caused you to say, she or he is the one? 51
- Tell me about a time when you were able to resolve a difficult difference of opinion, so that the outcome pleased you both. 51
- Without being humble, what are the strengths you believe that you personally bring to the marriage? 51
- What are the qualities you see in your partner that will strengthen the marriage? 51
- What, to you, is the essence of your relationship, the part of who you are that makes your relationship what it is? 51
- Imagine it is 30 years from now, and you have a stable and happy marriage, a model of cooperation, mutual respect and love. Describe the three things that made it possible. 51

Partnerships, High Quality (Catholic Relief Services)

- Tell me about a high point — a time when you felt you were involved in a really good partnership, a time that stands out as significant, meaningful, mutually empowering, or particularly effective in terms of results achieved. Share the story. What made it a good partnership? How were you involved? What were the key learnings? 19
- Yourself: Without being humble, what do you value the most about yourself [in terms of what] things you bring to building high-quality partnerships? 19
- Your Society and Culture: Every society or culture has its own unique qualities, beliefs, traditions, or capabilities that prepare us for building good partnership relations. What two to three things about your culture or society are you most proud about in relation to qualities that might enhance or help build good partnerships? Can you share a story about your culture that illustrates its best partnership qualities? 19
- Your Organization: What currently are your organization's best practices, skills, values, methods, or traditions that make it ready to be a good partner organization? 19
- As you think about what it takes to build high-quality partnerships, especially across organizations from different cultures, what is the core life-giving factor in such partnerships, without which good partnerships would not be possible? 19
- If you had three wishes for this partnership, what would they be? 19

Power:

- What are your goals for this academic year? What are your personal goals? What will you do, and how will you be, to accomplish these goals? 48

Promotion of Justice (CHAC)

The Christian tradition views healthy relationships, the protection of individual human rights, and the common good as basic to a healthy, peaceful and just society. It emphasizes the link between promoting health and working to overcome injustice. The vision of the Catholic health ministry seeks not only to respond to sickness and suffering, but also to counter the causes of injustice. 32

- Share an experience you had or witnessed that exemplifies justice being lived in the Catholic health ministry. 32
- What enabled that experience to happen? What was it about you, the other people with you, the organization, the situation, etc? 32

Spirituality at Work

- Tell us about a time when you felt most alive, most purposeful, most excited about your work. Who or what made it so? What were the most important factors about the organization that helped to make this a vital experience? 57
- How have ethics played a role in this experience? 57
- As a leader, what resources do you rely on to stay inspired in your work and your ongoing development? 57
- What are the personal/spiritual practices you have found most useful? 57

Strategic Planning, Springfield Dominicans: Parable Conference

- What positive impact have the goals of Parable had on you personally? 42
- How has Parable impacted Dominican Life within the order? 42
- What about the work of Parable do we want to carry into the future? 42
- What are areas around which we need creativity, new ways of meeting needs? 42
- What will Parable look like in 2010? 42

Traditions

- Focusing on the executive council as a living entity —an entity that has a history of enabling traditions as well as a potential future capability that is yet to be developed. Please tell me which of the council's traditions have been most life-giving and tell me a story of one time when that tradition was enacted. 62

Vibrant Parish Life / Spiritual Reflection

- How is God at work in our diocese right now? 55
- What is God asking of us in our place and time? 55
- How is God at work in my life right now, and what is God asking of me? 55
- How can I as an individual and we as a group more fully serve the reign of God? 55
- Tell a story from your own experience that best illustrates the application of this commandment to love one another. As you reflect on that incident, what is the most important thing you learned from it? 55
- We develop our understanding of God's Word over time, gradually learning deeper meanings and applying it to our lives. Right now, what does the passage mean to you? What could lead you to an even deeper understanding? 55
- Imagine that in the future you have taken this passage to heart and learned to love others as Jesus has loved you. What difference would this make in your life? In the life of your loved ones? 55
- In the future, we will continue to learn about how to apply these words to our own faith community. If there were one small step you personally could take toward loving others within our parish, what would that small step be? 55
- What most gives life to our parish? 67

- What would you like to see happen to bring forth the best of life and vitality in our future? 67
- When you are feeling best about your membership in our parish today, what image of parish life comes to mind? 25
- What is the single most important thing our parish has contributed to your life? 25
- Describe what is most nourishing and life-giving about our celebration of the Eucharist. 25
- What can you envision our parish doing in the next two to three years to call you and our people to an even fuller experience of the Eucharist? 25
- Think of a time when you participated in an educational or spiritual growth opportunity at our parish that really made a difference in your relationship with God. Tell the story of this experience. 25
- How can we improve our efforts to provide Catholic education and faith development in ways that would really help our faith become more alive and a part of daily life for you and your family? 25
- What do you see in our parish outreach efforts that have been of real service to people, and an inspiration to you? How can we more fully be of service to the neighborhood and broader community, particularly in partnership with others (other parishes, faith communities, community groups, etc.)? What exciting possibilities can you envision? 25
- When have you felt most welcomed and included at our parish? What in particular did people say or do that made you feel welcomed and included? How can our parish be much more welcoming to parishioners, to inactive parishioners or visitors? 25
- Think of a time when you participated in a worthwhile educational, spiritual, or social opportunity at a neighboring parish. What was the activity and where did it take place? What in particular did you most appreciate about this activity? What could we do to foster greater cooperation between neighboring parishes? 25
- In your opinion, what are the two to three best resources and greatest examples of vibrancy in our parish? 25
- If you could imagine or transform our parish in any way you wished, what one to three things would you do to enhance its life and vitality? Can you envision any of the three wishes you have described being done cooperatively with another parish? Which programs or ministries? Which neighboring parishes? 25
- Since our last meeting, where have you noticed God at work in our ministry ? 68
- What did we as a group do well today (ask at the end of any meeting)? 68

Vision

- What are your hopes for Catholic Campus Ministry? What are the aspirations you have for yourself as a leader of the Catholic Campus Ministry community? 48

Welcome

As a parish, we value being a warm and welcoming community. We want to welcome all people — different people with different gifts — to fully participate in our worship, teaching, service, and ministry. 36
- Describe a time when you felt that we truly conveyed an inviting and welcoming community to people. What do we do best to welcome people to participate? 37
- As you look to the future, what can we do to really encourage more people to feel welcome and participate in parish life? 37

Wisdom

- What strengths and values do you bring to your leadership role? How do you express these strengths and values in your life? 48

Index

Index

Index

Acknowledgements

Special thanks to the people listed who took the time to talk about their experiences. Rick Krivanka reported his conversations for the Sisters of Notre Dame and Heart to Heart Communications sections. Tana Paddock interviewed Canadians at the CHAC conference. Due only to my own limitations, this is not a complete list. Those listed are in no way responsible for the content but the book would be impossible without their generosity.

Fr. Gregorio Banaga, Sr. Shauna Bankemper, William Boomer, Marc Beaudry, Bernie Blais, Vanessa Griffin Campbell, Rev. Paul Chaffee, Rev. John Chlebo, Gayle Cilimburg, Sr. Margaret Crowley, Sr. Patricia Cuddihy, David De Lambo, Marlo Derksen, Rev. Norm Douglas, Br. Lawrence Fidelus, Mary Pat Frey, Sr. Jacquelyn Gusdane, Richard Haughian, Paul Hilt, Ralph Kelly, Lou Keim, Sandra Keon, Meg Kinghorn, Rick Krivanka, James Ludema, Michael Mayer, Therese Miller, Bernard Mohr, Fr. Martin Moran, Jennifer Nazaire, Warren Nilsson, Sr. Lisa Novak, Tom Osborn, Tana Paddock, Jacqueline Pelletier, Fr. Bernardo Pistone, Loretta Randolph, Ursula Remillard, V. Gail Roussey, Sr. Marilyn Jean Runkel, Terry Ryan, Michelle Smith, Helen Spector, Michel Thibault, Fr. David Turner, Maria Elena Uribe, Rev. Stephen Vellenga, Ronald L. Victor, Rev. Rob Voyle, Larry Vuillemin, Julia Wagner, Nancy Warden, Jane Watkins, Barbara Whitney, Pat Yankus.

Special thanks to readers of draft copies who were generous with their time and thoughts. Here is the group who agreed to let us acknowledge them in print:

Lia Bosch, Mary Ann Boyarski, Ed.D., Frank Campagna, Kathy Carmean, Judith Cauley, CSJ, Michelle L. Collins, Margaret E. Crowley, RSM, Ph.D., David Delambo, Ph.D. , Kathleen Duffy, Michelle M.C. Kocurek, Richard S. Krivanka, Donna March, Mary Ann McNally, Barbara J. Northan, Martha O'Brien, Elizabeth Pennewill, Rev. Bernardo Pistone, V. Gail Roussey, Ingrid Ruiz, Lucille H. Sansing, Maria Elena Uribe, Linda Foley Woodrum.

About the Author

Susan Star Paddock's years of experience as a psychotherapist to individuals, couples and families led easily into work with the larger "families" of organizations. Since learning Appreciative Inquiry, Susan has used it to help colleges, businesses, non-profits, professional associations and faith communities discover the power of quality relationships. A quietly charismatic individual with a cheerful personality, Susan inspires confidence, trust, and the courage to change in those who consult with her.

After many years of seeking, Susan happily converted to Catholicism. Her first book, *Mystic in the Marketplace: Turning Work into Worship* (IstBooks.com) compares the spiritual development of individuals with the spiritual development of organizations.

Susan earned her BA in Psychology from the University. of Missouri and her Master of Social Work at Temple University. School of Social Administration in 1975. She lives on a farm in Gettysburg, Pa. and can be contacted through www.catholicappreciativeinquiry.com.

Thin Book Publishing Co.

www.thinbook.com
888.316.9544 (phone)
888.331.8966 (fax)

Appreciative Inquiry in the Catholic Church   *$12.95 each*
- by Susan Star Paddock

Lessons from the Field: Applying Appreciative Inquiry   *$28.00 each*
- edited by Sue Annis Hammond, Dr. Cathy Royal

The Thin Book of® Appreciative Inquiry   *$7.95 each*
- by Sue Annis Hammond

The Thin Book of® 360 Feedback: a Manager's Guide   *$10.95 each*
- by Michelle LeDuff Collins, Ph.D.

Shipping will be added. See the website for details.

Credit Card Account No._____
(American Express, VISA, Mastercard)

Expiration Date_____

Name:_____

Company Name:_____

Address:_____

_____

_____

Phone:_____   Fax:_____